17/3/20X

JENKINS, S.
Get **more** out of libraries

728.8094281

Please return or renew this item by the last date shown.
You can renew online at www.hants.gov.uk/library
Or by phoning **Hampshire Libraries**
Tel: 0300 555 1387

 Hampshire
County Council

Discover
Britain's
historic
houses

Southern England

Discover Britain's

Published by Reader's Digest Association Ltd
London • New York • Sydney • Montreal

Reader's Digest

historic houses
Southern England

Simon Jenkins

Contents

4 WILTSHIRE

1 DORSET

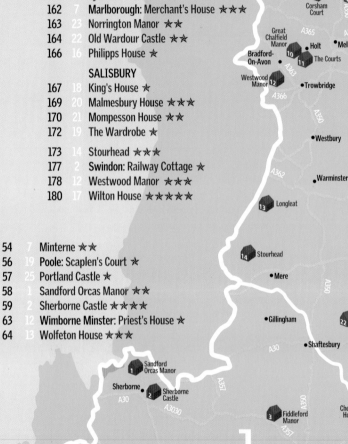

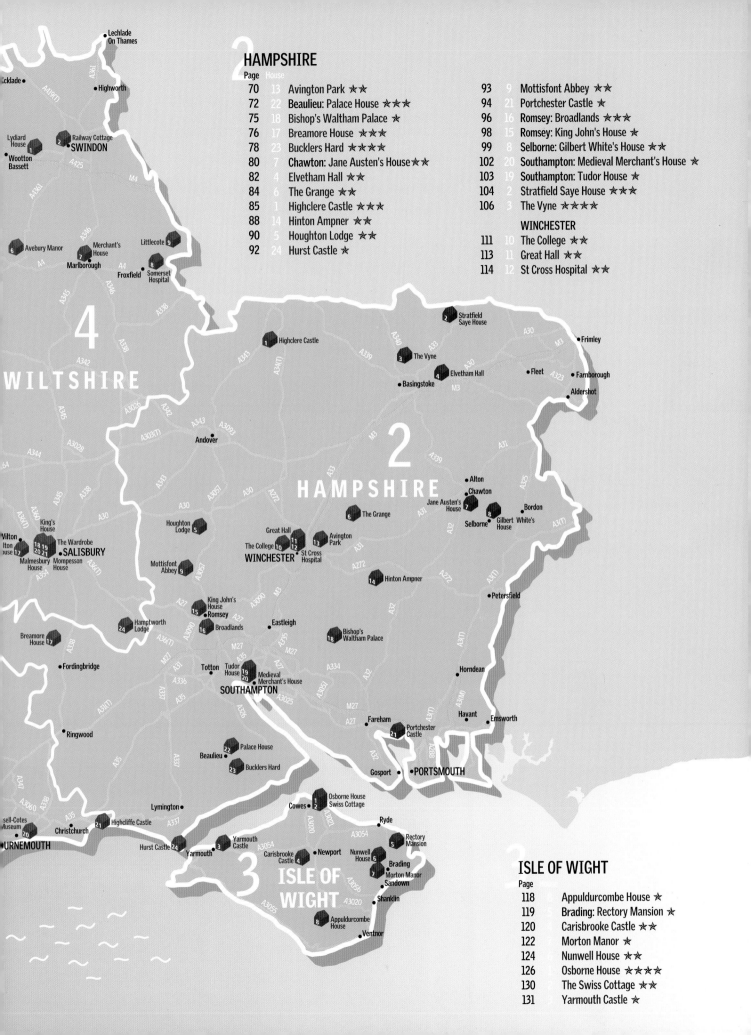

The best in Britain

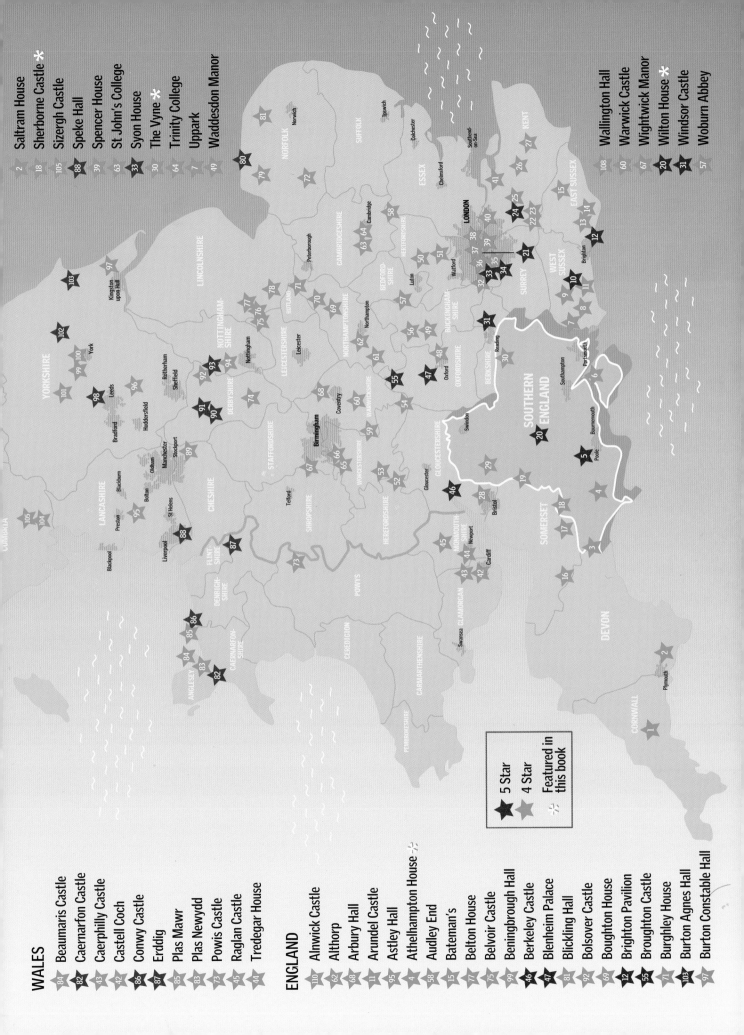

WALES

84	Beaumaris Castle
82	Caernarfon Castle
43	Caerphilly Castle
42	Castell Coch
86	Conwy Castle
87	Erddig
85	Plas Mawr
83	Plas Newydd
73	Powis Castle
45	Raglan Castle
44	Tredegar House

ENGLAND

110	Alnwick Castle
62	Althorp
68	Arbury Hall
11	Arundel Castle
95	Astley Hall
4	Athelhampton House ✳
58	Audley End
15	Bateman's
77	Belton House
75	Belvoir Castle
99	Beningbrough Hall
46	Berkeley Castle
47	Blenheim Palace
81	Blickling Hall
92	Bolsover Castle
69	Boughton House
12	Brighton Pavilion
55	Broughton Castle
71	Burghley House
103	Burton Agnes Hall
97	Burton Constable Hall

2	Saltram House
18	Sherborne Castle ✳
105	Sizergh Castle
88	Speke Hall
39	Spencer House
63	St John's College
33	Syon House
30	The Vyne ✳
64	Trinity College
7	Uppark
49	Waddesdon Manor
108	Wallington Hall
60	Warwick Castle
67	Wightwick Manor
20	Wilton House ✳
31	Windsor Castle
57	Woburn Abbey

Key

★ 5 Star
★ 4 Star
✳ Featured in this book

I visited these buildings after writing a book on English churches and the experience was as moving as it was different. While places of worship were built according to the authority and liturgy of the Church, people built houses for themselves. A house was useful first and beautiful second, and from this derives the joy of visiting houses. They are a conversation between utility and beauty down the ages.

For me this was a voyage of discovery, and in defining the word 'house' I soon found that I could not sensibly distinguish castle from palace, house from hut, roof from ruin. My list embraces any structure in which men and women have laid their heads, provided that they are in some degree accessible to public view. The selection is a personal list and the commentary is a personal vision, warts and all.

Simon Jenkins

Historic houses
of Southern England

Dorset is rich in scenery. It is a landscape of hills and combes that roll in waves towards the sea, greeting it in cliffs of chalk and limestone. Dorset has one of the most diverse geologies in England, yielding hard Portland stone and Purbeck 'marble' in the south, blue lias and Ham stone to the north and west. Its villages are pretty, its market towns relatively unspoilt.

There are few better counties in which to study 16th and 17th-century architecture. The 16th-century abundance includes Athelhampton, Mapperton, Sandford Orcas and Wolfeton, the last being a fascinating transition to English Renaissance. Elizabethan merged into Jacobean at Sherborne, home of Walter Raleigh and then the Digbys. The Prideaux alterations to Forde are a delightful marriage of classic to medieval.

The 18th century is eccentrically Baroque at Chettle, Picturesque at Milton Abbey and sternly

Palladian at Kingston Maurward. The Victorians were more confident. From exile, William Bankes planned his stately treasure house of Kingston Lacy in the 1840s, and Bournemouth saw the concept of the Grand Tour updated at Russell-Cotes House. One of the last great country houses was built by Norman Shaw at Bryanston. Dorset has writers' shrines aplenty, with the Hardy houses round Dorchester and Lawrence of Arabia's eccentric Clouds Hill.

Hampshire shared with Kent and Sussex the frontline against invasion, but its wooded hinterland was harder to penetrate than points east, and the chalk uplands were less rich. Medieval kings met in the Great Hall at Winchester Castle and bishops at Bishop's Waltham. Other pre-Reformation remains can be seen at Winchester's College and St Cross Hospital, both superb examples of collegiate domestic architecture. The 16th century left two significant works, Breamore and The Vyne.

Charles II began a new palace at Winchester and the rooms prepared for him at Avington survive. The dazzling 18th-century Gothick interiors by John Chute have been restored at The Vyne. There is Georgian literary vernacular aplenty, from Jane Austen's House at Chawton to Gilbert White's delightful enclave at Selborne. The 19th-century Picturesque movement is represented in the cottage ornée of Houghton and the Grecian splendour of The Grange. The county moves into higher gear with Charles Barry's aristocratic Highclere. On the **Isle of Wight** romantic Carisbrooke Castle dominates the centre of the island. The Baroque façade of Appuldurcombe is also, sadly, a ruin, but Prince Albert's retreat at Osborne still charms.

Wiltshire's landscape can lay claim to the oldest settlements in England. Apart from the temples at Stonehenge and Avebury, little of this survives, but we sense it in the majestic curves of Salisbury Plain, the largest untilled chalk downland in Britain. The county was one of the richest in medieval England. A contemporary said its wild uplands 'could sustain an infinity of sheep'. In the 15th and 16th centuries, the flanks of the Cotswolds rolled bales of wool into the watermills of the Wiltshire valleys. Until the 17th century it was the most industrialized part of England, dominated after the Dissolution by three grandees, Herbert of Wilton, Thynne of Longleat and Sharington of Lacock.

Of early Wiltshire, we still have the manors of Avebury, Great Chalfield, Norrington and Westwood, classics from the 15th and 16th centuries. Their rescue in the Edwardian era was one of the triumphs of early conservation. They are surpassed by two of the most impressive Elizabethan houses in England, Littlecote and Longleat, a supreme work of the early English Renaissance. Wilton is the best surviving work attributable at least in part to Inigo Jones, with its Single and Double Cube Rooms now splendidly restored. From the late 17th century are the gracious mansions of Salisbury. Palladian Georgian is represented by Stourhead and by sad Bolingbroke House at Lydiard. Late-Georgian classicism is seen at Philipps House.

The county was not a centre of Victorian activity, except for Crace's interiors at Longleat, but the Edwardians did more than restore old manors: at Hamptworth, Jacobethan was refreshed with the finest amateur craftsmanship.

★ STAR RATINGS AND ACCESSIBILITY ★★★★★

The 'star' ratings are entirely my personal choice (but see note below). They rate the overall quality of the house as presented to the public, and not gardens or other attractions. On balance I scaled down houses, however famous, for not being easily accessible or for being only partly open.

The top rating, five stars, is given to those houses that qualify as 'international' celebrities. Four stars are awarded to houses of outstanding architectural quality and public display. Three-star houses comprise the run of good historic houses, well displayed and worthy of national promotion. Two and one-star houses are of more local interest, are hard to visit, or have just one significant feature.

Accessibility varies greatly, from buildings that are open all year to houses that can only be visited 'by appointment' (rarely, I have broken my rule and included a private property that is not open at all, but is viewable from nearby walks or public gardens). Opening hours tend to alter from year to year, but an indication of how accessible a house is to visitors is given at the start of each entry, together with brief information on location and ownership. Many of the houses are National Trust or English Heritage properties, some are now museums or hotels, others are privately owned by families who open to the public for part of the year (English Heritage grant requirements insist on 28 days minimum). Some owners may, understandably, seek to cluster visitors on particular days. More details for each house are given at the back of this book, and readers are advised to check before visiting.

A final note, houses are, or should be, living things subject to constant change and how we view them is bound to be a subject of debate. I welcome any correction or comment, especially from house owners, sent to me c/o the publisher.

NOTE: On the UK map (pages 6-7) the 4 and 5-star houses in England and Wales were selected by Simon Jenkins. Those in Scotland were selected by Hamish Scott and the editors of Reader's Digest.

Architectural timeline
and houses of Southern England in brief

Appuldurcombe House
The ruin of a great Baroque mansion. Built at end of 17th century by unknown architect in the style of Wren and influenced by Vanbrugh. Set in Capability Brown landscaped grounds.

Athelhampton House
A late 15th-century house built in Ham stone. The Great Hall features spectacular beams and an impressive Gothic bay window with stained glass.

Avebury Manor
A 16th-century manor house, probably built around an earlier monastery, much restored in the Edwardian era, when the topiary garden was created.

Avington Park
Home of one of Charles II's courtiers, adapted as a private retreat for the King in 1670. The classical portico is painted wood, masquerading as stone.

Beaulieu: Palace House
Once the gatehouse of a Cistercian monastery, converted to a manor house after the Dissolution, then remodelled in Victorian Gothic-revival style.

Bishops Waltham Palace
The ruins of the palace of the Bishops of Winchester. Built in the 12th century and then rebuilt in late English Gothic at the end of the 14th century.

Bournemouth: Russell-Cotes Museum
Built at the turn of the 20th century as a home for the Russell-Cotes and their collection of artefacts. A combination of Scottish and Italian styles, with unusual turrets.

Bowood House
The remains of a house by Henry Keen and Robert Adam, home to a fine art collection. The Orangery and library preserve some of Adam's work.

Brading: Rectory Mansion
A Tudor mansion built around a courtyard. The interiors have been restored to their Tudor appearance, and peopled with waxworks.

Breamore House
An Elizabethan house made in aged red brick to a traditional E plan, the interiors restored after a 19th-century fire. An interesting art collection hangs on its walls.

Bryanston School
A late Victorian mansion in red brick with white stone dressings. An example of Richard Norman Shaw's version of Queen-Anne style, heavily influenced by Christopher Wren.

Bucklers Hard: Labourer's Cottage
The cramped accommodation of an 18th-century labourer's family, evidence of the meagre lifestyle of the poorest workers.

Bucklers Hard: New Inn
Reconstruction of a village inn, re-creating an evening out at the pub in the late 18th century.

Bucklers Hard: Shipwright's Cottage
The cottage of a skilled worker in the late 1700s, recapturing family life in the house at the end of the working day.

Carisbrooke Castle
A medieval fortress commanding an important strategic position overlooking the centre of the Isle of Wight. Castle walls enclose various buildings from several eras.

Chawton: Jane Austen's House
The 17th-century red-brick house where Jane Austen lived from 1809 until her death in 1817. Furnished with contemporary furniture and Austen memorabilia.

Chettle House
Originally believed to be the work of Vanbrugh, but now attributed to Thomas Archer. A red-brick, English-Baroque building with Archer's trademark rounded-off corners.

Clouds Hill
The simple woodland cottage where T.E. Lawrence stayed when not on duty at nearby Bovington Camp; this was his home when he was killed nearby in 1935.

Corfe Castle
A medieval fortress guarding the Isle of Purbeck, scene of a protracted Civil War siege. The most complete remains are the keep and those chambers known as the Gloriette.

Corsham Court
A late 16th-century house extended in the 18th century by Capability Brown, who also put up the Gothick bath house in the grounds. The north front is a Victorian copy of the south.

Dorchester: Hardy's Cottage
The thatched cob cottage, built in 1800, where Thomas Hardy was born. Furnished with simple country pieces and Hardy memorabilia.

Dorchester: Max Gate
An unremarkable late-Victorian red-brick house, made remarkable by its architect and first owner, Thomas Hardy, who lived in the house until his death in 1928.

Elvetham Hall
A Victorian house built by S.S. Teulon in high-Gothic style, complete with towers and turrets. The interiors are decorated with scenes from tales and legends.

Fiddleford Manor
A distinguished medieval hall house dating back to the 14th century and with some 16th-century additions; notable for the complex timberwork of the roof

Forde Abbey
A medieval abbey of great wealth and splendour, converted into a palatial mansion in the 17th century, fit for Cromwell's Attorney-General, Edmund Prideaux.

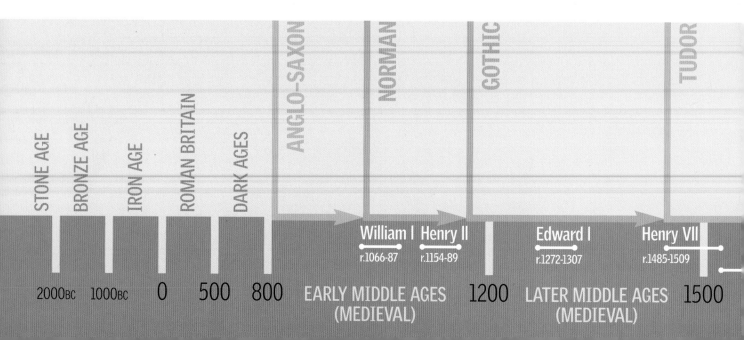

Froxfield: Somerset Hospital
An almshouse founded in 1694, still in use today. Built around a rectangular courtyard with a Regency Gothick chapel at its centre.

The Grange
The remains of a house by William Wilkins, an early example of the Greek-revival style, constructed in 1809 around an older, 17th-century building.

Great Chalfield Manor
A medieval manor house, complete with Great Hall, moat and gatehouse, built around 1470. Edwardian restoration work by Harold Brakspear.

Hamptworth Lodge
A Jacobethan-style house from the early 20th century by the architect Guy Dawber. A timber-framed building with steep gables and groups of tall chimneys.

Highclere Castle
A grand Victorian mansion, built by the 3rd Earl of Carnarvon. The work of architect, Sir Charles Barry, it reflects his other major project of the time, the Houses of Parliament.

Highcliffe Castle
An early 19th-century cliff-top house, adorned with stonework rescued from ruined medieval sites on the Continent. Ruined after a 1960s fire, the interiors remain unrepaired.

Higher Melcombe
Surviving wing of a 16th-century house, complete with attached former chapel. A fine plasterwork ceiling and linenfold panelling to be found inside.

Hinton Ampner
Originally a Tudor-style Victorian house that was remodelled on Neo-Georgian lines in the 1930s, Hinton Ampner was reconstructed in the 1960s after a fire.

Holt: The Courts
The classical Georgian façade of this house is an important focal point for the garden that surrounds it.

Houghton Lodge
A rare chalk-cob cottage built around 1800 that originally would have had a thatched roof. A fine example of the *cottage orné* style.

The monastic heritage

After the Dissolution of the Monasteries in 1539, former religious houses were put to new uses. Many urban monasteries became civic buildings, such as town halls or guildhalls, or were divided up into multiple dwellings. Large religious houses in rural areas often passed to individuals and became private homes, especially in the south of England, the Midlands and parts of the West Country. More often than not, the new owners were courtiers – Henry VIII gave many abbeys to his most faithful followers: William Herbert acquired Wilton in this way.

By tradition, a monastery or nunnery was laid out with the cloister, chapterhouse and dormitory occupying the eastern range, the stores in the western range and the refectory opposite the church. Buildings for lay brothers and workers, such as kitchens and guesthouses, were outside the claustral areas. Some new owners simply plundered these structures for materials and built afresh, but others converted them into the sort of homes they were more comfortable with. Houses with great halls, private apartments and service wings, usually ranged around a courtyard, were built up over the old monastic structures, incorporating bits of the old buildings. Some new owners, like William Sharington at Lacock Abbey, made minimal changes to the original layout and simply adapted the monastic buildings. Over time, subsequent owners made further changes. Often the original structure of a former monastery or nunnery, such as the Augustinian priory at Mottisfont, still lies hidden beneath the later additions.

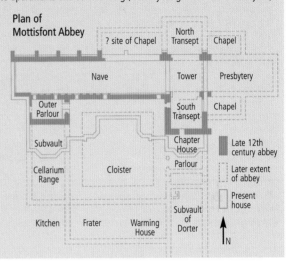

Plan of Mottisfont Abbey

Hurst Castle
One of the fortresses built by Henry VIII, in use until the 1950s. Begun in 1541, it guarded the entrance to the Solent. The original Tudor interiors survive.

Kingston Lacy
A 17th-century house by Sir Roger Pratt, altered in the 19th by Sir Charles Barry. Home to a magnificent collection of fine art and Grand Tour treasures.

Kingston Maurwood House
An early 18th-century house, built originally in brick and then clad in stone, reputedly in order to satisfy the tastes of George III.

Lacock Abbey
The Tudor conversion of a 13th-century convent that allowed much of the monastic structure to remain. Additions from the 18th century are some of the earliest examples of Georgian Gothick.

Little Clarendon
A medieval hall house, dating from the 15th century, with two-storey porch and solar wing, restored in the early 20th century.

Littlecote
A medieval house that was extended in the 1530s with an E-plan extension. A later red-brick, E-plan façade was added around 1600.

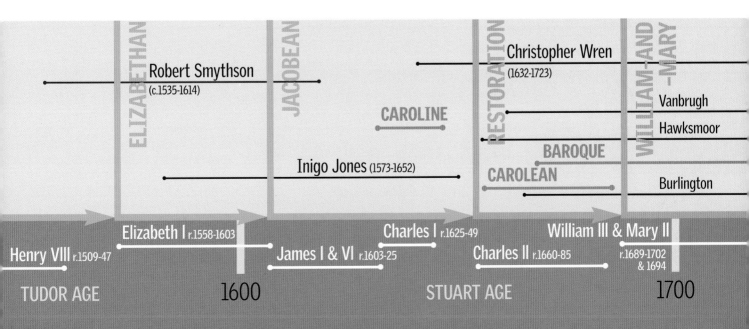

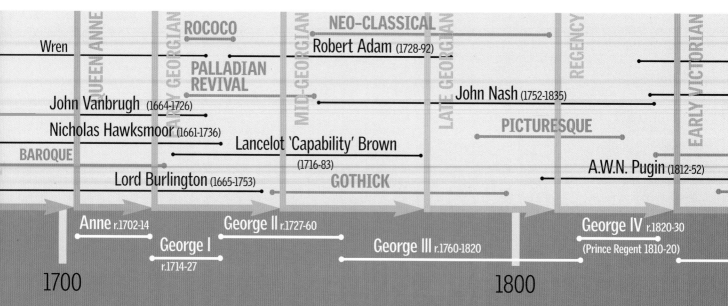

Ogee arch

Gothick style

The term Gothick with a 'k' has come to be applied to the earliest period of Gothic Revival architecture, beginning in the 18th century and lasting into the early 19th. It is also sometimes known as 'Strawberry-Hill Gothic' after the house of that name built by Horace Walpole, often regarded as the finest example of the style.

There is a discernible difference between Gothick buildings and those of the later Neo-Gothic style, also known as Victorian-Gothic. Neo-Gothic architects took an approach that could be described as 'archaeological', in that they were interested in reviving actual medieval forms of architecture. Gothick style was more concerned with adapting picturesque elements from buildings of the Middle Ages. Gothick architects employed copious decorative details, such as ogee arches, pointed doorways and crenellation, with little or no regard for the structural logic of the original medieval architecture – indeed, many Gothick buildings have classical proportions.

Gothick architecture was essentially an expression of the 'picturesque', an aesthetic movement that took pleasure in all things irregular and asymmetric. A Gothick-style folly provided an ideal focus in the 'naturalistic' landscaping that became so popular in the 18th century, such as Capability Brown's garden at Corsham Court.

Longleat
A sublime example of an English-Renaissance palace, begun in 1568. The interior was reworked by Sir Jeffry Wyatville early in the 19th century, and redecorated by J.G. Crace in the 1870s.

Lulworth Castle House
A Neo-Georgian, red-brick house of the 1970s, built in the grounds of Lulworth Castle as a home for the Weld family, after their castle was gutted by fire.

Lulworth Castle
Early Jacobean hunting lodge built on a grand scale, with crenellation and round towers at each corner. Ruined by a 20th-century fire.

Lydiard House
A Georgian Palladian mansion of the 1740s, possibly the work of Roger Morris. Inside, fine Georgian decoration and plasterwork remains.

Mapperton
An Elizabethan mansion, much extended in the 17th century, and with Georgian alterations and redecoration. Surrounded by gardens of a formal design.

Marlborough: Merchant's House
A silk merchant's town house, built after Marlborough's fire of 1653. The interior is in the process of being restored to its 17th-century appearance.

Milton Abbey School
A medieval monastery converted into a mansion in the 1770s by Sir William Chambers in a Picturesque adaptation of Gothic style, set in a Capability Brown landscape.

Minterne
A 1904, Arts-and-Crafts house by Leonard Stokes, built in an outwardly Tudor style but showing the influence of other eras throughout.

Morton Manor
A manor house of many parts, some medieval, some Tudor and some dating from the late 17th and the 18th centuries. Furnished with an eclectic antique collection.

Mottisfont Abbey
An Augustinian abbey with Tudor and Georgian additions, surrounded by a famous rose garden. Inside is a room with *trompe-l'oeil* decoration by Rex Whistler.

Norrington Manor
A medieval hall house, added to over time; a 17th-century wing forms the living quarters today. A solar wing and Tudor stair tower can be seen.

Nunwell House
A house begun in the early 17th century and added to regularly since then. To the rear is a 17th-century façade; to the front, is Georgian.

Old Wardour Castle
A medieval fortified mansion built on a hexagonal plan and extended in the 1570s. In the 18th century it became the focal point in a Capability Brown landscape.

Osborne House
An Italianate palace designed by Prince Albert as a retreat for his family by the sea. Victoria and Albert's personal rooms remain as they were during the Queen's lifetime.

Osborne House: The Swiss Cottage
Cottage built in the grounds of Osborne House in the style of a Swiss chalet as a superior sort of Wendy house for the Royal children.

Philipps House
Built by Sir Jeffry Wyatville in 1813, under the influence of Sir John Soane, a classical-style house with only the simplest of architectural decoration.

Poole: Scaplen's Court
A medieval merchant's house near the quayside, made up of four ranges and built around an inner courtyard.

Portchester Castle
The remains of an ancient castle, dating back to Roman times. The castle keep within the inner bailey is the only part still roofed.

Portland Castle
Built overlooking Weymouth Bay in 1539 as one of Henry VIII's chain of fortresses that were designed to protect the towns and ports of England's south coast.

Romsey: Broadlands
A Palladian house set in parkland, designed by Capability Brown in the 1760s with portico by Henry Holland. Inside is magnificent stucco work by Joseph Rose.

Romsey: King John's House
A mid-13th-century building that became used as a cottage and claimed as King John's hunting lodge. With rubble and flint walls and the curiosity of a floor of animal bones.

Salisbury: King's House
The medieval palace of the abbots of Sherborne. An original staircase is found inside, and a fine Jacobean geometrical plasterwork ceiling.

Salisbury: Malmesbury House
A William-and-Mary mansion, with Georgian redecoration, currently being restored.

Salisbury: Mompesson House
An 18th-century urban mansion with Baroque frontispiece. The interior rooms are traditionally Georgian, dating from the 1740s, and include a staircase hall with stucco-decorated walls.

Salisbury: The Wardrobe
A medieval mansion that was once a bishop's storehouse. The façade was rebuilt in the 15th century but parts date back to the 13th. Unusual Rococo decoration is found inside.

Sandford Orcas Manor
A mid-1500s house built to an unconventional plan. Other than a few 17th-century alterations, the house has remained little changed.

Selborne: Gilbert White's House
A medieval hall house adapted and extended in the 18th century by the naturalist, Gilbert White, and surrounded by the gardens he designed.

Sherborne Castle
Sir Walter Raleigh's hunting lodge, extended and adapted by later owners, the interiors revamped in the 19th century.

Southampton: Medieval Merchant's House
Built in around 1290, this town house has been returned to how it would have appeared as a house and wine shop in the mid-14th century.

Southampton: Tudor House
The town house of a 15th-century wealthy custom's official. The hall with screens passage and gallery is still in evidence.

Stourhead
Begun in the 1720s, this is an early example of English Palladian architecture by Colen Campbell. It is surrounded by one of the finest landscaped gardens, laid out in the 1740s.

Stratfield Saye House
A Jacobean house owned by the Pitt family and much altered by them both inside and out during the 18th century. It became the home of the 1st Duke of Wellington.

Swindon: Railway Cottage
A preserved railway worker's cottage, part of a model village built in the 1850s for workers on the Great Western Railway, designed by Sir Matthew Digby Wyatt.

The Vyne
A Tudor house that has been classicized at various points in its history. Early Gothick additions and Victorian restorations can also be seen.

Westwood Manor
An L-shaped medieval manor house, much refurbished in the 17th century. Antique panelling and internal porches rescued from elsewhere were added in the 20th century.

Wilton House
A Palladian palace by Inigo Jones and John Webb begun in the 1640s with interiors by James Wyatt in the early 19th century. Most notable among the grand state chambers is Jones' Double Cube room.

Wimborne Minster: Priest's House
A 16th-century town house with remaining medieval hall. A clothier's shop in the 18th century, it became an ironmonger's, now re-created at the site.

Winchester: The College
A collection of medieval buildings arranged around courtyards and designed to house academics and scholars; founded in the late 14th century.

Winchester: Great Hall
The 13th-century Great Hall is all that remains of Winchester Castle. A 14th-century, painted wooden roundel, known as 'King Arthur's Round Table', hangs at one end of the hall.

Winchester: St Cross Hospital
Almshouses founded in 1136 as a refuge for the poor and infirm, and still in use. Most of the buildings seen today, set around courtyards, date from the 1440s.

Sir Charles Barry

Charles Barry (1795–1860) was born in London, the son of a stationer. He was apprenticed to a surveyor at the age of 15, but when his father died he inherited a legacy that enabled him to travel abroad to study architecture. Between 1817 and 1820 he journeyed through France, Italy, Greece and the Middle East, sketching buildings of interest.

After returning to England Barry began work as an architect, at first designing mainly churches, then moving on to public buildings. Heavily influenced by the architecture of Renaissance Italy, he came to develop a style he called 'Anglo-Italian', which was first clearly evident in his design for the Travellers' Club (1830) and later in the Reform Club (1837). In 1835, he redesigned Kingston Lacy (Dorset) as an Italian palazzo in the English countryside.

By the time Barry was commissioned by Lord Carnarvon to design Highclere Castle (Hampshire) in 1838, he was already working on his most celebrated project: the Houses of Parliament. After the Palace of Westminster was gutted by fire in 1834, a public competition was held to select the architect for its replacement, and Barry was the winner. He worked on the building – with A.W. Pugin – for over 20 years, bringing his Italianate influence to an essentially Gothic building. He was knighted in 1852.

Wolfeton House
A manor house of medieval and Elizabethan origins. Much of its grandeur dates from the late 16th century and includes fine plaster ceilings and carved wood decoration.

Yarmouth Castle
The last of the Henrician coastal forts to be built, completed in 1547, a partner to Hurst Castle on the other side of the Solent. Features an unusual square bastion.

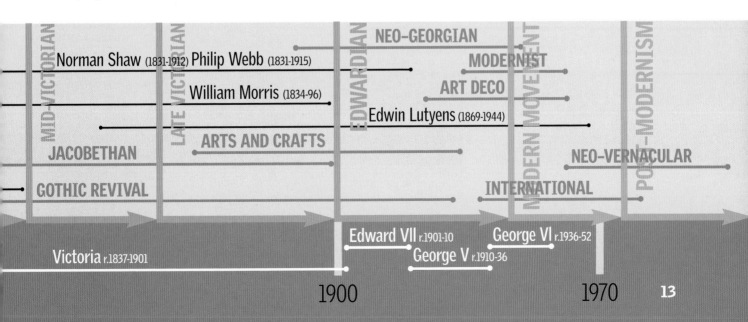

MID-VICTORIAN
Norman Shaw (1831-1912) Philip Webb (1831-1915)
LATE VICTORIAN
William Morris (1834-96)
EDWARDIAN
NEO-GEORGIAN
MODERNIST
ART DECO
Edwin Lutyens (1869-1944)
ARTS AND CRAFTS
MODERN MOVEMENT
POST-MODERNISM
NEO-VERNACULAR
JACOBETHAN
GOTHIC REVIVAL
INTERNATIONAL

Edward VII r.1901-10
George VI r.1936-52
George V r.1910-36
Victoria r.1837-1901

1900   1970   13

Dor

Sherborne Castle

set

Dorset

Athelhampton house

★★★★ Restored early Tudor mansion that retains much of its original character

Near Athelhampton, 6 miles NE of Dorchester; private house and gardens, open all year

Athelhampton is rightly celebrated as a medieval gem, glowing with promise on the main road out of Dorchester. Its Tudor windows and generous gables, its Ham stone walls, and gardens like something from *Alice in Wonderland* suggest an age of galleons and furbelows. Here, the past greets the present in easy embrace.

Medieval houses bear restoration either lightly or heavily. Athelhampton's is so light that it is hard to know it is restored at all. Yet it is, and drastically so. The house was built by a wealthy merchant, William Martyn, after the

Battle of Bosworth in 1485. It was given its generous west wing half a century later. For a full century after that it froze, as a result of being bequeathed in equal parts to four daughters in 1595. Each was told to occupy exactly a quarter of the property. This version of Continental partigeniture had the effect of preventing alteration but denying maintenance. When the desperate place was finally united in 1848, seven successive ownerships ensued.

Salvation came with a wealthy purchaser, Alfred Cart de Lafontaine, in 1891. By then

'The **hall roof** is sensational.'

Left Magnificently cusped beams and carved timbers grace the roof of the Great Hall at Athelhampton, just as they have since the room was first built in the 15th century. More finely carved wood in the form of linenfold panels was introduced later to adorn the walls. The Gothic windows include panes of 16th-century heraldic glass that chart the family alliances of the Martyns, Athelhampton's original owners.

Above The King's Room is on the site of the original solar of the 15th-century house. It is now furnished as a bedroom, featuring some early 17th-century carved oak furniture, such as the coffer and tester bed. **Below** The Martyn ape appears in the window of the Great Hall; the family motto was 'he who looks at Martyn's ape, Martyn's ape shall look at him'.

the old gatehouse had been demolished as derelict, which opened up the forecourt to the road. Lafontaine rebuilt the south wing to the right of the hall and laid out the garden. In 1957, the Cooke family, whose son, Sir Robert, was an MP and historian of the Palace of Westminster, bought the house. The property and gardens are now owned by his son, who clips the famous yew pyramids himself.

Athelhampton's pride is its surviving Great Hall, to which is attached a magnolia so large as to make us wonder which is upholding which. The hall roof is sensational. The beams form giant cusps, almost clover leaves, and are beautifully tooled and corbelled. The bay window is worthy of a Perpendicular church, rising almost the height of the hall. It has its own stone vault and exterior battlements. The screen and the linenfold panelling come from elsewhere, courtesy of Lafontaine, and a fine tapestry has been hung on the wall.

Heraldic glass includes the Martyn ape, the family emblem derived from the Church's 'second naming of animals' (the monkey was Martin and the fox Renard).

The King's Ante-room off the bay leads through to the Great Chamber in the west wing, its ceiling and panelling again introduced by Lafontaine. Next door is the old wine cellar, a little too scrubbed but a rarity in a house of the period. Lafontaine's library above doubles as a billiard room. Its equipment and rules date from 1919. The scene is adjudicated by a stern bust of Queen Victoria.

The so-called King's Room reflects the house's status; it is where the manorial court was held in the name of the King. Again, the restorers have introduced linenfold and a Gothic fireplace. Many of the recent furnishings and wallpapers at Athelhampton are derived from A. W. N. Pugin's work at the Palace of Westminster, of which Sir Robert Cooke was an ardent restorer. The chairs are Pugin designs. In the centre of the room is a model of Big Ben. The rooms of the south wing are either Victorian restoration or new building. The staircase was boldly reinstated after a bad fire in 1992.

The gardens, designed by Inigo Thomas, were created by Lafontaine and have been maintained ever since. The famous Great Court is created from giant yew hedges and peopled with pyramid yews like a guard of honour.

Below The formal gardens at Athelhampton were laid out between 1891 and 1899. The Great Court, the largest area of the gardens, is dominated by twelve tall pyramids of clipped yew – each one about thirty feet – that edge a sunken lawn. At the centre is a formal fishpond and in warmer months a fountain emerges from the marble basin.

Bournemouth: Russell-Cotes museum

★★☆ Victorian tycoon and collector's cliff-top mansion

Russell-Cotes Road, Bournemouth; museum, open all year

The Victorian houses of outer Bournemouth were, to William Morris, 'blackguardly and suitable only for ignorant purse-proud digesting machines'. This was dangerous talk, since many of their occupants were Morris's patrons. One such was the builder of East Cliff Hall, a local hotelier and mayor, Sir Merton Russell-Cotes. He presented this house to his wife, Annie, in 1901 and to the town in 1907. The architect was a local man, John Fogerty, but the inspiration throughout was Sir Merton's. He wanted the house 'to combine the Renaissance with Italian and Scottish Baronial styles'. He later declared that it was only 'after spoiling various plans my ideas were realized at last'.

The house might be in a rich enclave anywhere from Glasgow to Deauville. Its two conical towers and central pavilion gaze over the cliff to Bournemouth pier. A bold balcony below leads down to a pretty Japanese garden. The interiors are sensationally 'over the top', but executed with such bravura, and filled with such enjoyable paintings, that all can be forgiven. This is Bournemouth's Brighton Pavilion.

The house is entered from the road at the upper floor. This makes a visit seem like descending into Valhalla. A huge central hall runs from top to bottom, its skylight alive with the signs of the zodiac. The house is a riot of colour. The balcony railings are in green and

Above An elaborate *koro*, an incense burner, in the form of a silver elephant; a collection of Noh theatre masks; and fine examples of Samurai armour and weaponry – some of the highlights among the Japanese treasures in the Mikado room.

black. A frieze on the staircase depicts the Elgin Marbles. Every available inch of wall-space has a painting, mostly of the Victorian and Scots Romantic period. They have such titles as *Caledonia, Stern and Wild* or Landseer's *A Flood in the Highlands*.

Since the house is now the central section of a museum and art gallery, the bedrooms are no longer displayed as such. Yet there is no museumitis. The rooms were built to display the objects brought back by the Russell-Coteses from their constant travels, many of the rooms reflecting a single visit. Some people bring back

photographs. Russell-Cotes brought back roomfuls of antiques and curios.

Upstairs are the Mikado Room from Japan, a Moorish Alcove inspired by the Alhambra, and a room dedicated to the couple's friend, the actor Henry Irving, including the skull he always used in *Hamlet*. The quality of decoration is astonishing, with care taken over the embossing of flax wallpaper, the hanging of oriental lanterns or the arranging of Staffordshire china in a display case. And always there is the sea below, reflecting light onto the ceilings. Here Victorian is never gloomy.

Bryanston school

The school is open only by appointment but the grounds, courtyard and terrace can be perambulated. Bryanston was one of the last large country mansions to be built in England. Its architect in 1889 was Richard Norman Shaw and his client the 2nd Viscount Portman, owner of much of Marylebone. The house took five years to build but was occupied by the Portmans for just thirty years before it became a school. The approach is somewhat spoiled by school buildings.

This house is Shaw in his last, most emphatically Queen Anne phase. It is almost a parody of Sir Christopher Wren. The best view is from the A350 across the valley to the south-east. From here the house appears to rule over the landscape like a feudal palace, secure in its plantation. Closer to, the entrance front dramatically embraces three sides of a courtyard. The façade is alive with rustication and opulence. It must be a fearsome place to arrive on a first day of school. The red bricks with white stone dressings were once black, but are now restored and sparkle in the sun.

At the rear, the garden front is no less bold. The composition appears to be of a central mansion with two lesser ones paying court on either side. The window surrounds are aggressively rusticated and the roof is steeply hipped, with giant chimneys. Steps descend grandly to the hillside below. The interiors have been institutionalized, though the central hall is a tremendous space, soaring to the roof.

Chettle house

★ ☆ Fine example of an English Baroque house by Thomas Archer

At Chettle, 6 miles NE of Blandford Forum; private house, open part year

Chettle sits on Cranborne Chase and was built by the Chase warders, the Chafin family, who had bought the estate under Elizabeth I. Their commission was to ensure that the open moor and woodland 'remain in a flourishing state until the general dissolution of all things'. They contrived to succeed in this onerous charge until 1818. Chettle was then sold to the Castleman family, bankers from Wimborne. Their descendants, the Bourkes, occupy and maintain it to this day.

The house, begun in 1710 and twenty years in the building, is most unusual. It was attributed to Vanbrugh until opinion settled on his assistant, the gentleman architect, Thomas Archer, designer of St John's, Smith Square in London. It is in a wayward English Baroque, a style that emerged briefly under Sir Christopher Wren and disappeared with the Hanoverian succession and the rise of formal Palladianism. Chettle thus represents something of a stylistic blind alley.

The house is of redbrick with rounded corners and a high parapet. The rounded corners,

also seen at St John's, Smith Square, seem obsessive. The projecting centre of the garden front has them, as does the house itself. The entrance front is wonderfully strong, with giant pilasters dividing each bay and deep arched windows in the centre. Two curving flights of steps lead up to the door, continuing inside the entrance. They seem to draw the visitor ever upwards. On the wall are old hats worn by Chase warders.

Only a few rooms are open to the public. The most magnificent is the central hall. This has two superb oak staircases rising on either side and coming together in a gallery, a thrilling Baroque composition. There are three balusters to each step.

The drawing room was redecorated, as was much of the house, by Alfred Stevens in the 1840s. The style is a rather fey French, quite unlike the roast beef of Thomas Archer outside. The Bourkes are now valiantly refurbishing the rooms.

Clouds hill

☆ Simple cottage home and refuge of T. E. Lawrence

Near Bovington Camp, 9 miles E of Dorchester; National Trust, open part year

Clouds Hill is unlike any other house in this book series. Were it not for its former owner, it would be an insignificant two-up, two-down cottage by a road under a hill. Yet it distils in brick and stone all the sands of Arabia and the romance of war. It also distils the laceration of self-doubt and the solitude of introversion. In May 1935, 'Aircraftman Shaw' died in a lane nearby, thrown from his Brough Superior motorbike four months after retiring from the services. He had swerved to avoid two cyclists. Thus died Lawrence of Arabia.

Lawrence's exploits in the desert during the First World War, when in his twenties, were well recorded (by himself), including his tying down of a huge Turkish army and his chaotic three-day rule in Damascus. Afterwards he went into retreat. He wrote his memoir of the campaign,

Thomas Edward Lawrence
1888–1935

Before the First World War, T. E. Lawrence spent many years in the Middle East, studying archaeology and learning the language and customs of the Arab people. When war broke out, he was recruited by British Military Intelligence to liaise with Arab insurgents as part of a campaign to encourage revolt against the Turkish empire. His role in the ensuing rebellion earned him the sobriquet 'Lawrence of Arabia'.

Above When Lawrence was at Clouds Hill he had little time for domesticity – he ate tinned food or dined out – and so he converted the kitchen into a Book Room. He lined the walls with his valuable book collection and designed the steel book-rest for his armchair for evening and winter reading in front of the fire.

grandly called *Seven Pillars of Wisdom*, worked briefly in intelligence, then vanished. He re-entered the services and flitted from the Royal Air Force to the Tank Corps and back to the RAF. He did so, said Basil Liddell Hart, 'for the same reason that thoughtful men in the Middle Ages went into a monastery' – or possibly to protect his homosexuality. He demanded anonymity and the most junior rank. He worked quietly for thirteen years until his retirement at the age of forty-six, shortly before his death. He was a pioneer of flying boats.

Lawrence rented the cottage at Clouds Hill in 1923, while serving (as 'T. E. Shaw') at neighbouring Bovington Camp. He had to sleep in barracks and used the house only for leisure. It became his home whenever he was not on duty, although he regarded it as 'ugly as my sins, bleak, angular, small, unstable, very like its owner'. There is no electricity and candles are everywhere. The cottage is utterly simple, its placidity spoilt only by a noisy adjacent road. Over the door is a Greek inscription, translated as 'Why worry?'

There is little to see at Clouds Hill. Downstairs is the Book Room and a small bathroom. The former contains Lawrence's divan and the steel reading desk which he designed himself. The wall-racks have books about Lawrence and copies of ones he owned, as well as photographs he took in the desert. They seem a world apart from this place.

The two rooms upstairs are the music room and a bunkroom. The first contains an old gramophone, a typewriter and second-hand Lawrence works on sale. The bunkroom was kitted out for guests as a ship's cabin, with bunk and porthole. E. M. Forster slept here. It was 'papered' in aluminium for dryness and thus used to store cheese, as it still does. Sir Alec Guinness, who played Feisal in the film *Lawrence of Arabia*, donated an Arab robe. A habitation intended to be most ordinary is really most strange.

Corfe castle

⭐ Romantic ruins of a Norman and medieval fortress

6 miles SE of Wareham; National Trust, open all year

Corfe may be in ruins, but they are the ruins of England's most romantic house-fortress. The site is superb, guarding the road to the Isle of Purbeck. In its outer bailey, knights might joust away their fortunes. Beneath its rampart, troubadours might sing of love. This is pure Walter Scott.

The old Norman castle belonged to the Crown until awarded by Elizabeth I to her favourite, Sir Christopher Hatton. His family sold it in 1635 to the Lord Chief Justice, Sir John Bankes. It was the scene of a celebrated Civil War incident in 1643 when defended by Lady Bankes on behalf of her husband who was away fighting for the King. Lady Bankes signed a temporary peace with the surrounding Parliamentary forces, but used it to provision and refortify the castle.

The subsequent siege lasted six weeks, against over a hundred attacking troops. When the latter withdrew, Lady Bankes again refortified the castle and, with her husband now dead, faced another siege in 1645. A gallant Royalist platoon offered to rescue her but she refused. The castle finally fell to treachery, but Lady Bankes was allowed to keep the keys to Corfe in recognition of her bravery. Corfe was 'slighted' and the family later moved to Kingston Lacy (see page 43), where the keys still hang.

The castle is easy to read, rising up the hill from an outer gatehouse. The outer bailey's battered walls form a picturesque sequence of tumbled masonry, delighting 19th-century watercolourists. The inner bailey was first fortified in the 11th century. The principal buildings left standing are the 13th-century keep and the complex of residential chambers known as the Gloriette. The castle today is mostly of the 13th and 14th centuries, although some Gloriette windows and doorways are Tudor. Walls and passages survive, notably between the keep and its south annex. The great Gothic windows of the Gloriette hall retain their arches. Visitors can still climb the bastions from which Lady Bankes's defenders gazed down on their besiegers below.

Protagonists in the 'scraping' debate can compare guidebook photographs of Corfe in the 1940s and 1950s, covered in ivy, trees, weeds and nature, with its present scrubbed neatness. It is soon to undergo repointing to prevent more deterioration of the 12th-century lime mortar.

'Beneath its rampart, troubadours might sing of love.'

DORCHESTER
Hardy's cottage

★ Country-cottage birthplace and home of Thomas Hardy

At Higher Bockhampton, 3 miles NE of Dorchester; National Trust, open part year

'The little thatched house is as Hardy would recognize it.'

The point is not the cottage, nor that Thomas Hardy was born and spent his youth here. The point is the setting. The little thatched house is as Hardy would recognize it. Wild flowers abound in the garden, 'such hardy flowers as flourish best untrained'. The lane to the cottage, half a mile from the car park, is unpaved and sandy. Beyond the house is a crossroads of tracks, also unpaved, beneath a fingerpost sign – most Hardyesque. If only the distant traffic noise were reduced and the Forestry Commission could be induced to plant fewer conifers.

The cottage was built by Hardy's great-grandfather in 1800. It was of cob – a mix of clay, gravel, sand and chalk with straw – thatched and later strengthened with cement and faced with brick. The rooms are simple, with Hardy memorabilia downstairs and three modest bedrooms upstairs. It was in the middle one that Hardy was born in 1840. He was put aside as dead until the nurse remarked, 'Stop a minute, he's alive enough.'

At the window in the end bedroom, shared with his brother, Hardy wrote *Under the Greenwood Tree* and *Far from the Madding Crowd*, both filled with vignettes drawn from the immediate surroundings. The young Hardy wrote incessantly. When he found himself inspired and without paper, he would seize slates, strips of bark, even leaves, to capture the words.

Few writers left so many images of their childhood and few houses so evoke those images. In the poem 'Domicilium', the 16-year-old Hardy recalled how the 'Wild honeysucks/ Climb on the walls, and seem to sprout a wish ... / To overtop the apply-trees hard by.'

The rooms are as uneventful as they always were. They have kept their cottage state, with flagstones downstairs and old bedroom furniture upstairs. Books, drawings and watercolours abound. It was Hardy's family home until he married, at the age of thirty-four, and he still walked out here from Max Gate in Dorchester to see his surviving relatives. When the last member left in 1916, the house was tenanted until being acquired by the National Trust in 1948.

Thomas Hardy
1840–1928

Hardy began writing while still a boy, inspired by the countryside around his home. He continued to write during his career as an architect until the success of *Far from the Madding Crowd* allowed him to concentrate on literature. His novels captured an England before industrialization and the modern age changed the countryside for ever. Much of his work was set in the imagined county of Wessex, inspired by Dorset and the surrounding counties. Real places were disguised with different names – Higher Bockhampton, the hamlet where Hardy was born, became Upper Mellstock in his books.

Max Gate

★ House designed by Thomas Hardy as his Dorchester home

Alington Avenue, Dorchester; National Trust, open part year

Thomas Hardy was a writer by occupation but an architect by profession. Many might disregard the latter after visiting the house he built for himself and his new wife, Emma, outside Dorchester in 1885. The contrast with his boyhood home at Hardy's Cottage could hardly be more stark. Max Gate is a suburban brick villa on what was an exposed site once occupied by a man named 'Mack'. Hardy phoneticized his entrance into Max Gate, and even suggested a punning 'porta maxima'.

It was here that Hardy's relations with Emma declined. Even when they moved in he was full of foreboding. 'Whether building this house at Max Gate was wise expenditure of energy is one doubt, which if resolved in the negative is depressing enough. And there are others.' Emma hated the place, complaining of its exposed location. Hardy planted 2,000 Austrian pines to shield it (they are now gone) but not surprisingly they made Emma gloomier still.

While Hardy enjoyed a social life and visited London for the 'season', Emma disliked society and preferred taking religious tracts round local village streets. She was deeply upset by her husband's overt atheism. After her death, Hardy 'fell in love with her' in remorse. His second wife and secretary, Florence, had to spend her time typing out posthumous love poems to her

predecessor. It was here he wrote his later works, including *The Mayor of Casterbridge, Tess of the d'Urbervilles* and *Jude the Obscure*.

The house is solely of interest because of Hardy. Its front was described by A. C. Benson, as 'at once mean and pretentious, with no grace of design or detail and with two hideous low-flanking turrets with point roofs', perhaps an excessively harsh judgment. The façade is asymmetrical, allowing ingeniously for a large drawing room to the right of the entrance and a smaller dining room to the left. On the wall is a sundial designed by Hardy with the motto *'Quid de nocte'*: What of the night?

Hardy memorabilia have been scattered between Hardy's Cottage, Max Gate and the Hardy Museum in town. I sense Max Gate did not get the best of the deal. Some furniture has been returned to help the tenants entertain visitors. The dark Victorian interiors that oppressed Emma have been brightened and filled with Dorset landscapes. The Grand Old Man of letters brought here a remarkable galaxy of visitors – Kipling, Stevenson, Yeats, T. E. Lawrence, Shaw, Barrie, Forster, Sassoon, Wells, Galsworthy and Housman. All seemed puzzled by what Virginia Woolf called this 'ordinary, nice, conventional, never-says-a-clever-thing' Englishman. She wondered how on earth she could write his obituary. If only walls could talk.

Fiddleford manor

⭐ Medieval hall house with original roof

At Fiddleford, 6 miles NW of Blandford Forum;
English Heritage, open all year

There are many challengers for the title of 'most spectacular medieval manor house interior in Dorset' but Pevsner awarded it to Fiddleford. The old building lies tucked away from the main road, adjoining what is now a private house. It dates from the 14th century and has been saved only by some miracle of man and agriculture.

The visible house consists of a truncated half of a hall plus a two-storey solar. The hall is open to the roof with boldly cusped braces clearly designed for decorative effect. The screens passage and solar were added in the 1550s by a Thomas White. He clearly wanted to give his house some style, including carved stone doorways behind the screen, leading to a pantry and buttery underneath the solar.

The solar's roof is c1380 and has beautifully carved members. There are fragments of wall-paintings and the ghost of a Gothic window.

Above In the solar at Fiddleford the roof is still supported by the original 14th-century carved beams. A contemporary wall painting that depicts the Angel Gabriel has also survived the centuries.

'The grounds overlooking Forde are a **tumble of terraces**, water gardens, temples and borders. **Go when the sun shines.**'

Forde abbey

★★★★☆ Monastic palace converted into 17th-century mansion

4 miles SE of Chard; private house, open part year, garden open all year

Forde is a house far too little acknowledged. It is the best example of a historic building frozen at that exhilarating moment in English history when the Middle Ages were passing into Reformation and belated Renaissance, when monastery was becoming palace. Forde is part medieval, part modern, part ecclesiastical, part plutocratic, and still in the custodianship of a private family.

Looking down from the hillside garden, the eye takes in at one sweep the story of this transition. A rambling, asymmetrical tableau embraces medieval and Cromwellian ranges, later joined under one continuous battlement. Yet each portion is distinct and full of interest. Behind them at right angles run two medieval wings, north and east, survivors of the great storehouses of the former abbey.

The last abbot of Forde was Thomas Chard. His Great Hall and ornamented entrance tower were of such princely lavishness as to spark an entire Dissolution of the Monasteries on their own. When the moment came, Chard personally surrendered his abbey without a fight and retired to become vicar of Thorncombe. The building passed through various owners, who plundered the old abbey church for stone.

Then, in 1649, the private quarters caught the eye of Cromwell's Attorney-General, Edmund Prideaux, who bought the buildings to refashion them as his mansion. He was said to have consulted the elderly Inigo Jones but his architect was probably Edward Carter, standing in for Jones as Surveyor of the King's Works during the Interregnum.

After Prideaux's death in 1659, his son was suspected of supporting the Monmouth rebellion. He escaped with his life and a huge fine from Judge Jeffreys, but the family fortunes never recovered. Forde went into a long decline, saving it from alteration through the 18th and 19th centuries. The house was acquired by the Evans family in 1863 who repaired it and passed it to their relations, the Ropers, who own it to this day.

Forde is entered under Abbot Chard's gatehouse porch. This is a supreme work of Tudor architecture, with friezes and window tracery of filigree delicacy. The Great Hall behind was truncated by Prideaux to create his new west wing. The hall must once have been vast. Prideaux also blocked the windows on the north side in order to insert a fireplace and staircase.

The stairs to Prideaux's state rooms are splendidly robust. A carved 'Spanish balustrade' is matched by a painted one on the wall dado. Carved wooden urns burst with flowers. The ceiling, like all Prideaux's insertions, is richly plastered, with plants intertwined with faces. This is the house of no Puritan. By the late 1650s, Cromwell's aides were clearly acquiring a taste for extravagance.

At the head of the stairs, the Grand Saloon is Forde's most sophisticated chamber. Its shallow-coffered ceiling is intricately plastered, the walls luxuriously panelled. On the walls hang a complete set of Mortlake tapestries, which were specifically ordered for this room and copied from the Raphael cartoons now in the V&A. They were confiscated by Judge Jeffreys but returned under Queen Anne.

Many Jacobean houses soon become a blur of tapestry and oak. Not so Forde. To walk down the Tapestry Passage is like being cloaked in gorgeous fabric. The Crewel Bedroom is filled with embroidery made by Ropers in the 20th century. The old upper refectory, now a library, is a curiosity. It was built by the Cistercians for those monks who wished to eat meat, but were required

Above Most of the alterations to Forde's medieval structure were made by Edmund Prideaux in the 1650s. In the Great Hall he had the north windows blocked, leaving the tracery clearly visible. **Left** More blocked windows have been found in the Saloon – once a medieval gallery – but these are now hidden behind the magnificent Mortlake tapestries that drape the walls. The Saloon's intricate plasterwork ceiling includes biblical scenes and Prideaux's arms at its centre.

to do so in a separate chamber from their vegetarian brethren. The screen at the south end is a Victorian insertion, apparently fashioned from 18th-century Breton bedsteads. The refectory chairs are covered in superb Dutch tapestry and look uncomfortable.

The enfilade of state rooms above the old cloisters is now a row of habitable bedrooms, all retaining their Prideaux ceilings. Each is furnished with some distinctive feature; doves carved in a door hood, three girls painted by Cuyp, a set of Devis watercolours, a damask

bed canopy made for Queen Anne, who died before she could use it. Beyond lies the former monks' dormitory, now pristine white. The adjacent undercroft makes a fine tea-room, its vaults patterned with Ham and Portland stone.

The Old Cloister was refaced and ornamented by Chard as one of his last acts as abbot. It is virtuoso Gothic and now is home to ferns and other vegetation, like a voluptuous orangery. The grounds overlooking Forde are a tumble of terraces, water gardens, temples and borders. Go when the sun shines.

Highcliffe castle

★★ Picturesque shell of a 19th-century castle built with imported architectural features

At Highcliffe, 2 miles E of Christchurch; private house, open part year, grounds open all year

Highcliffe is an architectural phenomenon on a bluff overlooking the Channel. In 1830 Lord Stuart de Rothesay, grandson of the 3rd Earl of Bute, inherited the Highcliffe estate, on which stood a cliff-edge mansion by Robert Adam. A much-travelled Regency diplomat who negotiated the end of the slave trade, Stuart decided to build himself a spectacular house in the new medieval revival style, looking out to sea and the Isle of Wight.

Antique hunters were at the time trawling the ruined medieval sites of a battered post-Napoleonic Europe to adorn English houses and churches. Few did so with the aplomb of Lord Stuart, who even insisted on putting a 'de' before his Scottish name of Rothesay. Twelve barges of Belgian stonework were duly brought to Highcliffe, most of it from the demolished Grande Maison des Andelys and the Norman abbey at Jumièges. An L-shaped house designed

Right The north window in the Great Hall is among the architectural gems from France that adorn Highcliffe Castle. Dating from 1547, it was originally in the church of St Vigour in Rouen. The window depicts the tree of Jesse, a representation of Christ's ancestry. Dismantled and kept in storage after fires damaged the castle in the late 1960s, the window was reinstated in 1998.

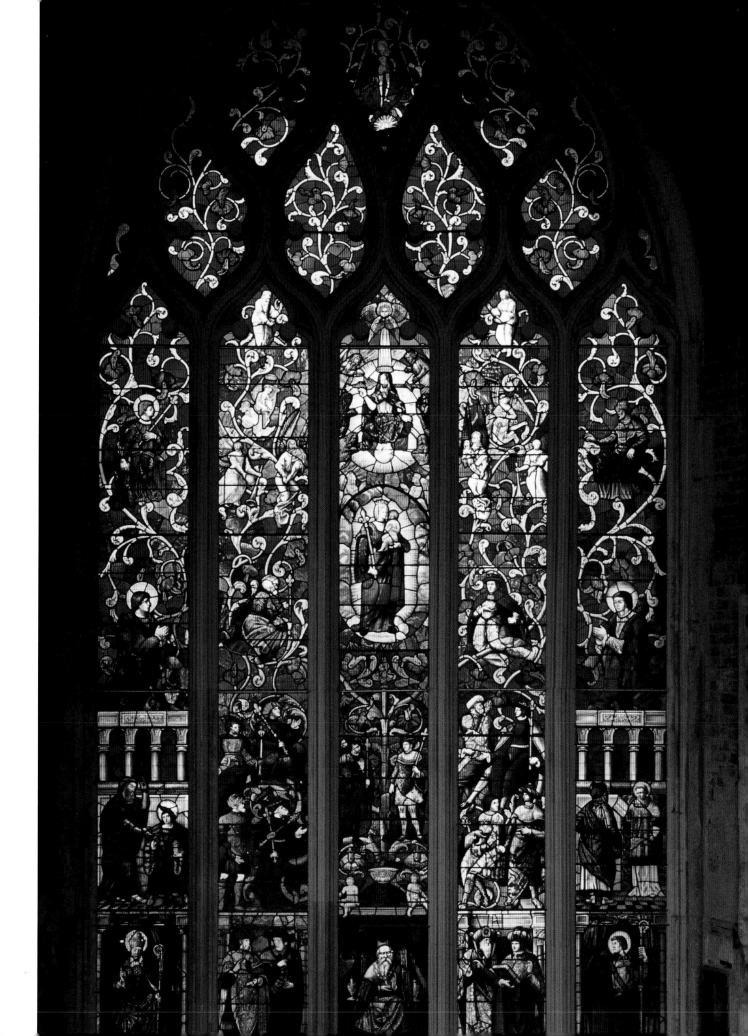

Above The King's Oriel window got its name because of a connection with French royalty. It once illumined a room at Grande Maison des Andelys where Antoine de Bourbon lay dying after the siege of Rouen in 1562. At his bedside knelt his son, the future Henry IV of France.

by John Donthorn, fearlessly inventive pupil of Jeffry Wyatville, was prepared for their reception.

The state rooms were in the south wing towards the sea, culminating in a large conservatory. The east wing was for the family. Behind was a Great Hall along the lines of the Great Western Hall at Fonthill, but filled with abbey stonework and with a sensational Gothic porch. Most magnificent were the oriel windows gracing the two towers of the rear entrance. Both are covered in Flamboyant Gothic tracery that would get Michelin stars were they on their original buildings.

All this was in good condition until 1950 when it was sold by its owners, the Stuart Wortley family. Brief use as a Catholic seminary was followed by two devastating and suspicious fires in 1967 and 1968. This left the interior of the building a ruin, from which nobody seemed keen to rescue it. The roof of the Great Hall fell as recently as 1990.

Acquisition by the local council and recent restoration is slowly bringing the building back to life, at least as a shell. Carved corbels, arches and windows adorn what remains of the Great Hall. The majestic double staircase that filled one end has sadly gone. The conservatory is in good condition. One of the castle's great treasures, the Jesse Window, has been put back into its orginal place in the Great Hall. In the grounds, historic paths and the view to the Needles have been restored.

Higher Melcombe

★ ★ Sixteenth-century manor house that incorporates a former chapel

Near Melcombe Bingham, 8 miles SW of Blandford Forum; private house, open by arrangement

The hills and valleys of central Dorset rise and fall seductively round the Melcombes. The valleys are lush but the hills are the wild, broad-shouldered heaths of Hardy novels. Climbing up from Cross Lanes a cul-de-sac opens out onto moorland through an avenue of limes, planted to celebrate the Battle of Britain. At the top of a combe, the road peters out in a small farm and what appears to be a chapel. The land was bought in 1938 by the brewing family of Woodhouse, including the old manor. It sits looking out on the Downs, solitary and beautiful.

The house was once four ranges set round a square. Much of this was demolished in the 18th century, the stone being used to build the Ansty brewery in a local village. What remains is an L-shaped mostly 16th-century house, its old rooms gently evolving over time. The walls are banded with flints interspersed with Ham and Portland, the two finest stones in England.

The interiors are essentially atmospheric. The earlier entrance front has walls of medieval thickness and the downstairs rooms have Jacobean chimneypieces. A staircase inserted in the 18th century leads to the old Great Chamber, now a bedroom with a superb plaster ceiling of c1610. It depicts the union of the crowns of England and Scotland. Another bedroom has worm-eaten linenfold panelling.

The former chapel, now a living room, was used as a barn by various tenants until restored by the Woodhouses. It has 13th-century windows, from a plague village church in the neighbouring meadow. Modern stained glass celebrates the love of nature of the present owner's grandfather. It includes the family (and brewery) emblem of a badger, also the name of its celebrated ale. The roof bosses have all been restored, including one of EII for the present Queen.

Kingston Lacy

★★★★☆ Italian-style palazzo housing magnificent fine art collection

2 miles NW of Wimborne Minster; National Trust, open part year

William Bankes was so wild, dissipated and adventurous as to shock even Byron, who called him 'my father of mischief'. Such was the scandal surrounding his life that Arthur Oswald, in his 1935 essay on the house, still dared not mention it. As a wealthy young man, Bankes travelled widely in Spain and the Middle East. He visited Mecca in disguise, returned to England and became an MP. With his new house in Dorset still a shell, however, Bankes was charged in 1841 over a homosexual incident and had to flee to Italy to escape arrest.

For the remaining fourteen years of his life he dreamed, collected, designed and directed the building of the house through his sister, Lady Falmouth. He was thought never to have returned, enjoying the house vicariously through correspondence. But family legend long held that, with Bankes's death approaching in 1854, a coach drew up one night at the gate of Kingston and a secretive figure slipped into the house to stand briefly in his beloved creation, and see the work of his mind's eye. This poignant story is now believed to be true.

The house was begun by Bankes's ancestors after their seat at Corfe Castle was destroyed in the Civil War (see pages 26-7). The architect was Roger Pratt and the present exterior is still a ghost of Pratt's work. Bankes had a vast inheritance at his disposal and wanted

Right William Bankes wanted Kingston Lacy to have a grand staircase, worthy of any Roman palace. His architect, Charles Barry, used clever tricks of perspective to give an illusion of greater space as the stairs rise up through the different floors and landings. He used Carrara marble for the treads; the balustrades are alabaster, capped with Biancone marble.

'Everything about the house is distinctive.'

Above The Great Parlour of Roger Pratt's 17th-century house became the drawing room in the 1780s. The ceiling was raised by Charles Barry in the 1830s. The room was decorated as it is seen today at the very end of the 19th century. **Right** The library is dominated by Guido Reni's superb large fresco, *The Separation of Night and Day*, dating to around 1600. In 2006, after more than twenty years of restoration, the National Trust was able to return the painting to its position on the library ceiling. **Above right** Sebastiano del Piombo's *The Judgement of Solomon*, painted around 1505, hangs in the dining room to the left of the organ. The panelling of oak and cedar comes from trees grown in the Kingston Lacy park.

something grander and more in the style of Italy. In 1835, he called on Charles Barry to redesign Pratt's house as a palazzo in which a Byronic European might display the spoils of his travels. Kingston was to become not just a house but a home fit for Velasquez and Raphael, Titian and Veronese, Rubens and van Dyck.

After Bankes's death, the house seemed to sink into a lethargy of shame. It passed from one reclusive Bankes to another until, by the 1970s, its inaccessibility was the stuff of legend. Then in 1981, out of the blue, Kingston Lacy was left by Ralph Bankes, lock, stock and barrel, to the National Trust.

Everything about the house is distinctive. Although ostensibly just another grand house filled with fine furniture and pictures, it everywhere displays eccentricity and surprise. The stairs, of white Carrara marble, reach the first floor past a loggia where are set three statues by Carlo Marochetti. They are of Sir John and Lady Bankes, heroine of Corfe, and their adored king, Charles I. This staircase was built before Bankes's flight and he declared that 'there is no staircase in England to equal it in effect ... and not many that surpass it in Italy'.

The first floor is the *piano nobile*. The library is a survivor from the 18th-century house. Over the fireplace are the keys of Corfe Castle, defended so vigorously by Lady Bankes during the Civil War. Above the bookcase is a set of family portraits by Lely and one by Batoni. The drawing room raises the temperature. Furnished as a cluttered Edwardian sitting room, its doors are surmounted by extraordinary carved marble architraves made in Verona. The portraits are by Lawrence and van Dyck and include a set of miniatures in enamel on copper.

The dining room has boxwood doors with carved panels, copied from a Donatello altar at Padua. On the wall hangs Kingston Lacy's greatest treasure, Sebastiano del Piombo's unfinished *Judgement of Solomon*, near-ruined by restoration, and a magnificent portrait by Titian. We now enter the saloon, mostly the work of Robert Brettingham in the 18th century. It contains Bankes's most important acquisitions. These include two luxuriant Rubens portraits, of Maria Serra Pallavicino with her parrot and of Maria Grimaldi with her dwarf. Other works are by van Dyck, Rembrandt, Titian, Veronese and Gerrit Dou, some of them 'studio of'.

Beyond is the Spanish Room, clad in tooled leather from Venice and with ceiling paintings copied from the Ca' Pisani on the Grand Canal. The gilding reflects subdued light. The art is Spanish and the room might be a sacristy in the Escorial. On the walls hang Velasquez, Murillo and Zurbarán. The state bedroom beyond is grandiloquent yet not cold. The bedstead is adorned with state cupids and state bats.

The marble staircase continues to the second floor, becoming yet grander as it rises. Nude figures after Michelangelo lounge on plinths. A vast Snyders of animal violence covers the wall. The upper floors are all bedrooms, many decorated by Barry and all lavishly adorned with Kingston Lacy's store of paintings. There is a Zoffany here, a Lely or a Kneller there.

We are able to penetrate deep into this house. The attics are lit by a cupola and adorned with an apse decorated with shells. The so-called Tent Rooms were intended for bachelors and are now immaculately refurnished.

The basement holds Bankes's collection of Egyptian antiquities, many of them removed from the workmen's village in the Valley of the Kings. This would be outrageous today. Nor is that all. On a visit to Egypt, Bankes took the obelisk from Philae and spent six years wrestling it home to his park. To England's shame, it stands there eroding to this day. Its uneroded twin stands on its temple island near Aswan, bereft of its partner.

Below The ceiling in the state bedroom features paintings bought by William Bankes once he had fled to live in Italy – four of the panels are attributed to the 16th-century artist Paolo Veronese. Bankes was never to sleep in the walnut and holly state bed, carved by Vincenzo Favenza, as he died before work on the room was complete.

Kingston Maurward house

⭐ A Georgian house in Portland stone, set in an Edwardian park

2 miles E of Dorchester; private house, now a college, is accessible by arrangement, gardens open part year

The house stands handsome across the valley of the Frome. Its Portland stone façade rises glittering in the sun from a dark mass of trees. The house was built by George Pitt, cousin of the Prime Minister, c1717 and was of brick. In 1794 it fell victim to a visit from George III, who is said to have wandered round it muttering, 'too much brick, Mr Pitt'. The King's dislike for this material proved advantageous to the Portland quarries. The result is an early Georgian box, nine bays by five, with pediments and entirely clad in stone. A porch was added in the 20th century.

The house and estate were occupied by the army in the Second World War and the building became a college, the Dorset Farm Institute. A farm exhibition forms a less than dignified approach, past rows of council houses. The main entrance hall, remodelled c1912, is accessible; it rises two storeys and has two giant imported fireplaces. The fine plaster ceiling, with a central oval and swirling Rococo decoration, has been picked out in bright colours.

The college has been restoring the splendid gardens over the years. Tall yew hedges and graceful terraces overlook a vista of lakes and trees, laid out in the Edwardian period. The garden contains the national collection of penstemons. There is a superb croquet lawn.

Lulworth Castle house

After the 1929 fire at Lulworth Castle (see page 48), the owner, Herbert Weld, was photographed sitting dazed among his belongings on the lawn. He had lost his wife to illness eight months earlier and had no children. Within six years he was dead and the estate passed to a cousin, Sir Joseph Weld, whose son holds it today. Sir Joseph decided that while he could not reinhabit the castle, he could live nearby, and in 1971 built a new house overlooking the site. It was designed to be light, airy and servant-free.

The house exterior is dull redbrick, the garden front (below) a rectangular façade punctuated by two spreading bow windows. The interior is more enjoyable, planned round a central hall rising two storeys and with a view to the sea framed by scagliola columns. Upstairs is a four-sided gallery with a barrel vault, hung with family portraits by Lely and others. In the dining room is an excellent tapestry based on Teniers, with his signature of a urinating peasant. It comes from a former Weld house, Ince Blundell Hall (Lancashire) where it is sorely missed.

The present owner, Wilfrid Weld, is a cricket enthusiast with an outstanding display of cricket memorabilia and commercial posters, warming the sometimes cold lines of 20th-century Georgian. Lead pipes, urns, statues and water butts retrieved from the old castle people the gardens of the new house. These merge with those of the adjacent castle. Most of the estate is open Dorset landscape, a blessed haven in the increasingly ruined Dorset coastline.

Lulworth castle

When the exiled King Charles X of France was lent Lulworth Castle in 1830 he is said to have exclaimed, *'Voilà, la Bastille!'* It is a good description. The castle was built 1608–10 by Viscount Bindon, a son of the Duke of Norfolk, near his seat at Bindon Abbey. With a spectacular view down to the coast, it was 'well-seated for Prospect and for Pleasure, but of little other Use'. The castle was an ostentatious hunting lodge.

In 1641, the estate was bought by Humphrey Weld whose family own it to this day. They furnished the castle and regularly modernized it, so that by the 20th century the ground floor comprised a hall, billiard room, dining room and large drawing room, with a Catholic chapel in one of the round towers. Lulworth well demonstrated the adaptability of every sort of English house.

In August 1929, a fire broke out in one of the towers. Molten lead spread across the roof which collapsed onto the floors below. The castle was completely gutted amid scenes of some drama. An ancient family ghost of a 'grey lady' was heard crying for help from a tower window and a ladder was even run up to rescue her (she, of course, had vanished). Old Herbert Weld, shouting 'My castle, it is ruined,' had to be restrained from rushing into the inferno.

For half a century the place remained a gaunt ruin, clad in ivy and with trees growing from its walls. It was taken ferociously in hand for the owners by English Heritage, who paid for and restored the exterior and consolidated the inside.

The outside looks as if it were built yesterday, a gleaming white keep set on a billowing basement of terraces and with a fine Renaissance doorway. Four corner towers are big enough to be keeps in their own right.

The interior is controversial. English Heritage inserted new floors, ramps for the disabled, strip lighting and ubiquitous hoardings and screens. The spaces bear no relation to their origins. Overhead hang the relics of the fire. Iron beams support bare walls. Fireplaces, doorways and fragments of stairs lead nowhere. Yet there is no sense of ruination, no vegetation, bats or birds. All is sparkling clean, and is now used also for concerts and private functions. It is a modern architect's fantasy of how a ruin ought to look.

The family chapel has been reinstated in one tower. The castle basement survived the fire and the Welds have created an admirable exhibition of life 'below stairs'. This is more real than life upstairs.

'The courtyard is **guarded** by two **splendid eagles,** looking ready for **take-off.**'

Mapperton

★ ★ ☆ Elizabethan house set in formal gardens

4 miles NE of Bridport; private house, open part year

Mapperton nestles on a flank of a private combe near the Devon border. It more than nestles, it glows, rich in Ham stone and rich in years. The years are those of a continuous line of descent from Domesday's de Moion family to the Comptons who sold the house in 1919. The present owner is the Earl of Sandwich, whose father, Lord Hinchingbrooke, bought Mapperton in 1955. Hinchingbrooke extended the formal gardens laid out in the 1920s by a previous owner, Ethel Labouchere, in memory of her husband.

The house presents a friendly face to the drive, although is easily missed on the way to the stables and outhouses. The exterior is that of an Elizabethan mansion of the 1550s, substantially extended in the 1660s and redecorated in the 18th century. A U-shaped courtyard is guarded by two splendid eagles, looking ready for take-off.

Beyond, the harmony of the lichen-clad stone and Elizabethan features is complete. To the left is the Tudor wing, with an attic gable and finials; to the right is the medieval chapel. Ahead is a porch with charming shell niches below an open balustrade. The atmosphere is intimate. Yet turn round and there is a spectacular view to open fields through symmetrical stable buildings, a surprisingly Baroque effect.

Given the simplicity of the exterior, the interior is hard to read. The cross passage, hall and dining room were re-ordered and given reproduction Jacobean ceilings in the 1920s. The overpowering Jacobean chimneypiece came, apparently, from another Dorset house. Old manor houses swapped and borrowed so freely that they often seem to merge into one panelled, ubiquitous, vernacular corporate design.

Abutting onto the hall is the drawing room, its original plaster ceiling rich in fleurs-de-lys. Beyond is the library, with a Rococo ceiling above a crude James I overmantel, again an import. Between the two rises the Georgian staircase, a spacious, stylish work with another Rococo ceiling. The walls are lined with Earls of Sandwich. They include the Restoration diplomat who brought back Charles II to his throne, and his descendant the 4th

Earl, who invented the famous snack by demanding a slab of beef between two slices of bread when in a hurry. The present Lord Sandwich is in the same business, claiming with due authenticity to market 'the original Sandwich'. Upstairs in the old great chamber is the finest ceiling in the house.

Below are spread out the gardens, billowing down the hillside in tiers of lawn and yew, intersected by arbours and Ham stone walls. The layout is unashamedly formal, yet fashioned in harmony with the contours of its site. Waves of landscaping seem to disappear downhill towards the wild, as if desperate to escape.

Below The Great Chamber at Mapperton is now used as Lord and Lady Sandwich's bedroom. The original pendant ceiling dates from around 1550 and the French four-poster bed, c1700, was believed to have once been owned by Madame de Maintenon, mistress of Louis XIV, the Sun King.

Milton Abbey school

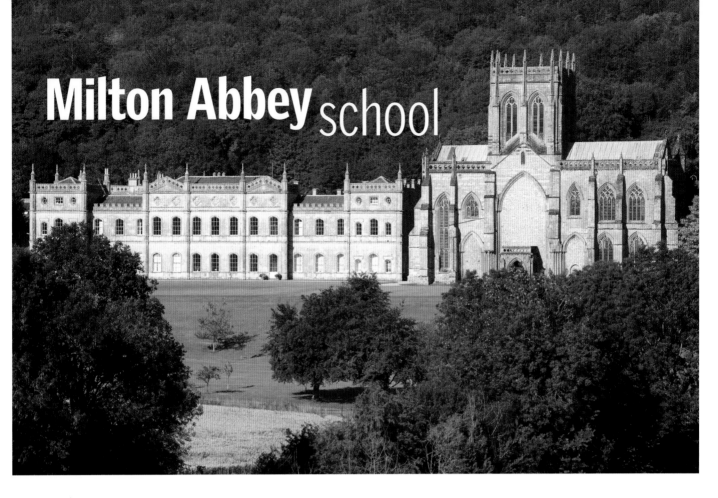

⭐ Eighteenth-century conversion of an abbey set in a Capability Brown landscape

At Milton Abbas, 8 miles SW of Blandford Forum; private school; Abbey church open part year

Towards the end of the 18th century, the Earl of Dorchester decided to wipe out the old village of Milton Abbas round the dissolved abbey. In ardent pursuit of the Picturesque, he created a new model village a mile away. The abbey church remained as a parish church, but the monastery next door was converted into a mansion. The interior, now a school, is not normally open but the walls can be perambulated and glimpses obtained of the inner courtyard.

The house is built round this courtyard, which retains the medieval Great Hall of the monastery and fragments of its walls. The hall is a superb structure with a vast hammerbeam roof and a flourish of cusped wind-braces. The original Tudor entrance faces north up the valley. To the west, looking across the valley, is the front built in the 1770s by Sir William Chambers and forming a delightful contrast to the abbey next door. It is intriguing that both are technically Gothic, the one true Perpendicular, the other best described as skin-deep Picturesque.

Chambers was predominantly a classical architect. The composition of his front is Palladian, a central block with two pavilion wings. The Gothic appears in nothing more than pierced parapets, pediments and finials. Except in the brightest sun, the grey Portland stone can seem cold alongside the church's honey-coloured Ham stone next door.

The architect later hated what he had done, calling Milton 'this vast ugly house in Dorset'. Historians suggest that the design was forced on him by his client. If so, it is a rare instance of an architect suffering such humiliation. The buildings do, however, sit serene in one of Capability Brown's most beautiful landscapes. The dominant colouring of Milton Abbey is neither Portland nor Ham, but the wide torrent of green that is the valley flowing past its front.

At Minterne Magna, 8 miles N of Dorchester; private house, open by arrangement, gardens open part year

The house at Minterne stands in a corner of paradise. The view from its terrace over the enveloping Cerne Valley is of water and park stretching towards woods and meadows. After buying the property from the Churchill family in 1768, Admiral Robert Digby would ride over to his relations at Sherborne, when Capability Brown was paying a visit there. He sought no costly commission. Digbys were their own landscape architects, but overheard ideas did not come amiss.

The present house was built in 1904 by the 10th Lord Digby. It is an accomplished Arts and Crafts work by Leonard Stokes. The design is ostensibly Elizabethan, with a modified E-plan entrance façade. Yet no sooner do we think we understand the plan than Stokes veers off into his own eclecticism. The doorway has a deeply curved hood (Queen Anne). The façades have rusticated quoins (Georgian), pedimented gables (17th century), fake castellation (Regency) and stone mullions to the windows (Tudor). There is an assertive tower, with Arts and Crafts windows (20th century).

The interior is even more eccentric. The door gives onto what appears to be a spacious screens passage and the hall with Gothic windows. But the Middle Ages come to an abrupt end when the screens passage becomes a spacious staircase up to a gallery. The hall has a classical arcade to a passage running down the middle of the house. One end of this passage is now a picture gallery of Digby portraits. Coats of arms and Digby cartouches fill the walls alongside seascapes of Digbys under sail. The hall is the scene of Lady Digby's regular musical patronage.

The three main reception rooms face out onto the garden. The dining room is a facsimile of an earlier 17th-century room on the site. It faces east to shield the Teniers tapestries from the sun. They had been given to Charles Churchill by the Dutch after the Battle of Ramillies and 'came with the house' on its purchase by Digbys. The large drawing room is wonderfully open to the view and is Stuart in character. The smaller boudoir is in the style of Adam.

To Stokes, it seems, Minterne was a place where anything would do except, apparently, bathing. The Edwardian Lord Digby considered bathrooms 'disgusting', leaving such innovation to his successors.

Minterne

'The house at Minterne stands in a corner of paradise.'

Poole: Scaplen's court

★ Surviving medieval merchant's house behind old quayside

Near The Quay, Poole; museum, open part year

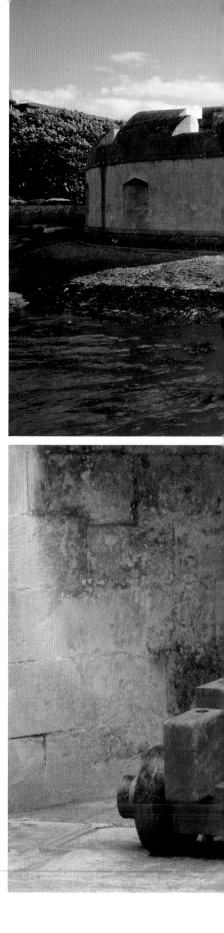

Poole has suffered even more from bulldozers than Weymouth. An almost intact ancient harbour survived both the Victorians and wartime bombing, but it could not survive Poole's local council. It has now all but vanished, leaving a tiny enclave round the Custom House on the old quayside. Behind it is Scaplen's Court.

This was a substantial merchant's house of *c*1500, of the sort that still abounds in Continental ports but is virtually extinct in Britain. It is a charming corner, composed of four complete ranges round a small inner courtyard. The original hall was to the left, with a solar block at right angles and service buildings beyond. The interiors are now used as an extension of the Waterfront Museum across the road.

Scaplen's Court, at the time of writing, is remarkable in being free of museumitis. The house seems full of Tudor and later paraphernalia, with the back rooms coated in cobwebs and dust. An upper chamber has a fine restored ceiling with wind-braces. This precious house has retained at least some sense of its antiquity. I hope it remains that way. Behind is a secluded garden, planted with old Tudor flowers and herbs.

Portland castle

★ Intact Henrician fortress

On Portland Harbour, 2 miles S of Weymouth; English Heritage, open part year

The photographer asked by English Heritage to find a good outside view of Portland Castle for the guidebook has excelled himself. The castle sits in a wilderness of defence ministry barracks, offices, sheds and hangars. The Royal Navy, so glamorous at sea, espouses unsurpassed ugliness ashore. Few of these buildings are any longer in use. Properly cleared, this could be a sublime spot, as the cleverly angled guidebook photograph indicates.

Portland is a complete Tudor fortress, built in 1539 to guard Weymouth Harbour as part of Henry VIII's south coast chain. It was reused during the Napoleonic Wars but converted in 1816 as a private house for the Reverend John Manning. His son, Captain Charles Manning, became governor of Portland in 1834. It was he who promoted the building of the great breakwater, using convict labour, to link what was then an island to the mainland. The castle was reactivated by the Navy in the 20th century and used in the Second World War as an Anglo-American communications base.

The castle is most curious in shape, an outer segment of a circle. Like many of these forts, it was essentially a gunnery platform, commanding a particular field of fire. The gun room is now open to the sky, its guns never having fired in anger. Behind it is the hall, a fine room with kitchens to one side and the gunners' living quarters the other. Upstairs are the officers' rooms, with the castle's only privy. Display panels depict scenes from the castle's history, including the Second World War. The view from the battlements is spectacular, strictly for visitors with tunnel vision, looking northwards.

Above Principal among the castle's defences was the single-storey gun room with embrasures for five guns, pointing out over Portland Harbour and Weymouth Bay.

Sandford Orcas manor

✭✭ Elizabethan manor with unusual hall

At Sandford Orcas, 2 miles N of Sherborne; private house, open part year

Sir Mervyn Medlycott Bt conducts tours of this ancient house with the air of a man baffled at anyone wanting to visit what is so patently his. Sandford has been in the family for two and a half centuries. Why should others be interested? Long may the paradox continue. The house is a manor of the mid-16th century, built by Edward Knoyle sometime after he acquired the property in 1533. Its plan and interior are unusual, but beyond that there is little to say. The house makes a virtue of lacking history.

The arched gatehouse with rooms above leads into the courtyard, but no building faces it, only a gently sloping garden. The house is round to the right, as if determined to be unobtrusive. From outside it seems a curiosity. The lovely Gothic porch, intricately adorned with foliage and finials, has on its left not the customary Great Hall with solar, but rather two rooms on top of each other, both with windows running round the front and side elevations. The so-called solar is a single-storey rear structure – in effect, a closet.

Inside, the hall is divided from the door by a sedate oak screen which must be Jacobean. It contrasts with the riotous carving of a mantelpiece, also Jacobean and possibly imported. The joy of the room are its windows, both carrying heraldic glass and, as seen outside, round two sides, flooding it with light and quite unlike a traditional Great Hall.

At the far end is no grand Tudor staircase but a simple spiral stair leading to the Great Chamber above. Sandford Orcas seems to have survived in this 16th-century state, with only a few later Jacobean additions, and did not suffer the often drastic attention of late-Victorian manorial improvers.

Although the house is quite small, the upstairs rooms are a maze of beams, steps and levels. There are few 'important' pieces of furniture, just the accumulation of a gentry family over the centuries. Atmosphere transcends artifice. Anything as recent as the 18th century – such as a lovely Hepplewhite bed – seems impertinently modern.

Sherborne castle

★★★★☆ Sir Walter Raleigh's hunting lodge, much altered by later owners

At Sherborne, 5 miles E of Yeovil; private house, open part year

Glamorous courtier, Sir Walter Raleigh, coveted old Sherborne Castle and in 1592 induced the elderly Elizabeth I to grant it to him. Unfortunately she soon discovered his secret marriage to one of her ladies-in-waiting and threw them both in the Tower of London.

On their release they retreated to Sherborne and began to rebuild the castle and the hunting lodge in its grounds. Raleigh's American adventures shattered his finances and James I returned him to prison in 1603 on charges of treason. By the time of his execution in 1618, the property had gone to one of the King's courtiers, Sir John Digby, later Earl of Bristol. Digbys abandoned the old castle and moved to and extended the hunting lodge. In course of time, it became Sherborne Castle.

Today, this building is one of the oddest houses in England. Raleigh's Elizabethan structure was pulled, pushed, distorted, rendered and set about with hexagonal towers. The original house was soon buried at the end of deep courtyards, while the side elevation to the park became eccentric. In the right light Sherborne is like a ghostly galleon, a Marie Celeste lost at sea.

'The library is ... a remarkable room, the bookcases alive with double-ogee arches and pierced with busts of philosophers.'

Below The library at Sherborne was remodelled in Gothick style in the mid-18th century by the 6th Lord Digby. The bookcases were created by master carpenter William Ride; the ceiling was designed by a local architect, Francis Cartwright. **Right** The green drawing room was originally the solarium and Great Chamber, the principal room in Walter Raleigh's time. The motto of the Earls of Bristol, *Nul q'Un* (None but One), is mounted over the fire.

In the middle of the building is still the ghost of Raleigh's house, with Tudor windows and a Dutch gable. This is flanked by blank walls and then two wings of classical windows that are reminiscent of a street in Florence. The building might be an architectural pattern book opened up and left in a meadow.

The interiors of Sherborne were mostly reordered by George Wingfield in 1859, when he inherited the property at the age of sixty, at the same time adding Digby to his name. A wealthy and generous 'improver', of whom Victorian Britain had an abundance, Wingfield Digby employed P. C. Hardwick to modernize Sherborne in keeping with its Jacobean past. Hardwick was so conscientious that here is a house whose Jacobean authenticity we must take on Victorian trust.

Of the interiors, the library is not by Hardwick but 18th-century Gothick of 1757. It is a remarkable room, the bookcases alive with double-ogee arches and pierced with busts of philosophers by Henry Cheere. A copy of my childhood favourite, *Struwwelpeter*, lies casually on a table. Over the

Right Lady Venetia Digby died suddenly in her sleep in 1633. This miniature of Venetia on her deathbed, painted by Peter Oliver and set in a mount of enamelled gold, was worn by her husband Sir Kenelm until his death in 1665.

Right Lady Venetia Digby died suddenly in her sleep in 1633. This miniature of Venetia on her deathbed, painted by Peter Oliver and set in a mount of enamelled gold, was worn by her husband Sir Kenelm until his death in 1665.
Below The internal draught porches in the Oak Room are a matching pair. They date from the 1630s.

fireplace is Sir Kenelm Digby, 17th-century Royalist, Catholic, scientist and cook. Son of the Gunpowder Plot Digby and cousin of the Sherborne branch, he fell in love with the penniless Venetia Stanley and was sent to France by his mother to escape so impecunious a match. He wrote passionate letters to Venetia but these were intercepted by spies. To escape an infatuated French Queen, he feigned his own death in battle. When news of this reached Venetia, she began a stormy affair with the Earl of Dorset. Hearing of this, an enraged Digby returned and married her in secret. They lived happily with their two sons until her early death in 1633.

The solarium is Raleigh's Great Parlour, with a stupendous Victorian marble fireplace and grand paintings of Victorian Wingfield Digbys. The Red Drawing Room is mostly original to the Digby house, its ceiling a gathering together of ostriches (the Digby crest) with roses, fleurs-de-lys, flowers and monsters. At one end is a processional painting of Elizabeth I attended by her courtiers. Here too is a copy of van Dyck's picture of Sir Kenelm with Venetia and their boys. We now wander through drawing rooms, boudoirs, bedrooms and turret rooms, each adorned with colourful fireplaces and flooded with light. They are also richly furnished. Sherborne is a treasure house of Georgian commodes, Boulle desks, lacquered cabinets and Owen Jones curtains.

A marked change in style comes with the descent to the old entrance hall. Suddenly we are back in Raleigh's hunting lodge. The fireplaces are rough, the arches of stone and the furniture of solid oak. The adjacent Oak Room retains two magnificent internal draught porches, crowned with a profusion of scrollwork. Below are Raleigh's original kitchens, hung with the usual copper but with an exhibition of curios, including Earl Digby's false teeth. They look painful.

Wimborne Minster
Priest's house

A town house with medieval hall and walled garden

High Street, Wimborne Minster; museum, open part year

This was a Georgian clothier's shop that became an ironmonger's owned by the Coles family. They left it to the town in 1987. The two-storey exterior is picturesque to the street and even more attractive behind, where it is of the same banded stone-and-flint that adorn the walls of the Minster opposite.

This ancient building has been altered, bruised, extended and filled in, but it is still recognizable. From the street, the gable was once a wing of a hall recessed from the street frontage, now buried behind a later shop front. The ironmonger's store has been reconstructed behind the façade, to what it was when it closed in 1960. Behind and to the left is the old house's parlour. This is panelled and restored to its appearance when the Kings, a family of mercers, owned the house in the 18th century.

Behind the re-created shop is the medieval hall, curtailed by the insertion of a staircase and partition. It contains a set of painted linen wall-hangings depicting the story of Joseph, of the sort found in many English houses that could not afford real tapestries. These are modern copies of the rare set at Owlpen Manor (Gloucestershire). Waxwork figures are discreetly arranged in these rooms – so discreetly that I could not tell them from two local ladies engaged in a lacemaking class.

Wolfeton house

★★☆ Medieval and Elizabethan manor with gatehouse

1 mile N of Dorchester; private house, open part year

Two bastion towers flank the gatehouse like a castle in the Dordogne. Old limestone walls seem under perpetual siege from nature. Inside are vaults unplastered, attics unconverted and windows uncurtained. Mention to Captain Thimbleby, the owner, that the place might be a French château and he erupts. A French château, he says, might be Wolfeton.

The house was home in the 15th century to a Dorset family, the Trenchards, to whom the Thimblebys are 'connected'. It was here in 1506 that Philip of Austria and his wife, 'mad Joanna', were brought one night by a Trenchard after being driven ashore at Weymouth. A young man called

'Old limestone walls seem under perpetual siege from nature.'

Above Wolfeton is entered by the north porch which leads into the passage, lined with linenfold panelling from the 16th and 17th centuries. The carved doorways, to the Great Hall and Parlour, date to the 1600s and include figures of Romans, complete with sandals and swords, and one of an ancient Briton brandishing a large club and draped in animal skins.

John Russell, known to speak Spanish, was summoned from Bridport as interpreter. He stayed with the couple on their way to Henry VI's court at Windsor, where he made such a mark as eventually to become Earl of Bedford and founder of the mighty Woburn clan. It pays to speak Spanish.

The two round towers of the gatehouse date from the early 16th century, one with a small chapel inside, the other with a spiral staircase composed of wooden blocks resting on their own weight, without a newel post. Beyond would once have been two courtyards, most of which fell down in the 18th and 19th centuries. Only the south range survives, plus an extraordinary Riding House of c1600, said to be the earliest such indoor riding school surviving in England.

Left The Parlour was rebuilt at the end of the 16th century and the overmantel features oak carvings of the period. Among the decoration are male figures said to represent the three degrees of man – knight, squire and servant. A series of wooden panels featuring the signs of the Zodiac – a complete set except for Leo – have now been moved from the Parlour and are on display in the Chapel.
Right The Great Staircase is not only unusual for the 16th century, it is believed to be unique – a similar stone staircase of around the same date built at Longleat no longer exists. It is claimed that the ghost of the family member who drove a horse and carriage upstairs for a bet has been seen on the staircase many times, repeating his absurd feat.

The south range is a handsome composition. Seen from the garden, the grand sequence embraces the circular gatehouse towers, a prominent staircase tower, the end windows of the Great Hall, a garderobe tower and then the three expansive 16th-century windows of the Elizabethan house, with a Great Chamber above. This runs the gamut from turrets, slits and battlements to Elizabethan stateliness.

The Great Hall windows merit an essay in themselves. They are irregular and cannot all be of the same date. What appear to be Perpendicular openings have Renaissance putti and mullions. One of these is even stepped outwards so as to suggest perspective.

The interior is a match for the exterior. The entrance is into a splendid passage with linenfold panelling, classical doorways and a 17th-century plaster ceiling. The Great Hall survives from the original building. It was heavily Victorianized but includes old panels and a magnificent doorcase. Fragments of Tudor carving include monkeys in human dress and a moustachioed man.

The two most remarkable rooms run along the Elizabethan wing. They have superb plaster ceilings with animals, masks and Red Indians. Even finer are the doorcases and overmantels, apparently moved here when other parts of the house were demolished in the 19th century. These rise the full height of the rooms and lend them great presence. The Parlour doorcase is nothing less than sensational, a giant Corinthian order framing a smaller order round the door itself. The fireplace carries attenuated sculpted figures in dark, rich wood. It had none of the crudity of many Jacobean pieces. The dining room beyond is less ornate, but again has an overmantel worthy of a palace.

Behind these rooms is a stone staircase, contemporary with the Elizabethan wing and lavish for a house of this period. A horse and carriage are said to have been driven up it. At the top is the doorway to the Great Chamber, a serenely classical work of *c*1590. The whole space, with its wide landing and doorway, might be in an Italian palazzo rather than an Elizabethan manor. It is attributed to craftsmen from Longleat (see page 154), where a remarkably similar staircase had recently been built. The Great Chamber itself is a large room recently restored, with a huge fireplace against its internal wall. This incorporates yet more Red Indians, sign of late-Tudor cosmopolitanism. The windows look out over the tumbled vegetation of the garden.

Hamp

Hampshire

shire

Beaulieu: Palace House

Avington park

★★ Charles II's retreat, with painted state rooms

At Avington, 4 miles NE of Winchester; private house, open part year

The Countess of Shrewsbury, mistress of the Duke of Buckingham, achieved notoriety by disguising herself as a groom and holding his horse while he killed her husband in a duel. She then married a prominent courtier, George Brydges. The association did Brydges no harm. He was a Groom of the Bedchamber and much involved in Charles II's frequent visits to Winchester, where the King was building yet another of his 'English Versailles'.

During one such visit, the Dean of Winchester had point blank refused to allow the King to lodge with his mistress, Nell Gwynne, in the Cathedral Close. It is possible that Brydges adapted his house up the Itchen Valley at Avington as a backstop.

Avington is the sort of English house on which Austen's Elizabeth Bennett might have gazed from afar and felt a flutter in her bosom. It is calm and magnificent, a Georgian villa set in a landscaped park. This is deceptive. Doubt surrounds the date of the impressive portico and

wings but it seems probable that they date from Brydges' alterations for Charles II. The portico appears to be of stone but is of painted wood and remarkably similar to Inigo Jones's St Paul's, Covent Garden. After a colourful life, Brydges died in 1713 trying to save his dog in the lake.

The house was next taken in hand by Brydges' successor, the Duke of Chandos, in the 1760s. He embellished it inside and put three statues on the portico. He also made plans to turn the house to the side and build a new wing to link it with its old banqueting house set across a yard at the back. This wing was aborted and remains only as a wall, a colonnade and two charming greenhouses. Avington's hind quarters are pleasantly picturesque. The house was bought by the Shelley family in 1848 and sold in 1952. It was then divided into eight apartments. The main rooms remain intact and are accessible.

The house interior appears to be mostly of the Brydges period. The entrance hall has paired wooden columns, like those of the portico. The

walls are later, painted to look like trellis work and the ceiling to look like sky. The artist was a Frenchman named Andien de Clermont who worked in the 1780s in a festive style known as 'singeries'. The staircase has honeysuckle climbing up the balustrade. Upstairs is the ballroom decorated by Chandos and remarkably grand for a building of this size. The panels of the seasons of the year, however, are attributed to Verrio and installed earlier, by Brydges' wife. The figure of Bacchus is prominent everywhere. This must surely have been intended as the monarch's private retreat.

Beyond the ballroom is a drawing room. The walls are by Clermont but adapted, some might say defaced, in the Regency period with panels depicting the royal dynasties of England. A superb mirror is from the lost Chandos house of Cannons Park in Middlesex, and is in Grinling Gibbons style. To the rear of the house is the library with a curved wall, a charming neo-classical room.

Above The drawing room walls are decorated with paintings of historical royal figures by Andien de Clermont; the Plantagenets run along the fireplace wall, the Tudors along the east wall. They may have been added to please the Prince Regent, the future George IV, who used to stay in the house. **Below** Clermont used several *trompe l'oeil* effects in his decorative scheme in the main hall – the pillars are painted to look like marble, but are actually made of wood.

Beaulieu: Palace house

★ ★ ★ Medieval and Victorian-Gothic house near the National Motor Museum

At Beaulieu, 7 miles S of Southampton; private house, open all year

In 1951, the twenty-five-year-old Edward Douglas-Scott-Montagu, 3rd Baron Montagu, inherited one of the many properties of the Duke of Buccleuch. A colourful man-about-town, Lord Montagu enjoyed old cars, jazz and high living. Above all, he loved Beaulieu, a house set in 7,000 acres of the New Forest. At a time when large country houses were embattling themselves against a grim future, he threw his house on the mercy of the public. Taking his cue from Longleat, he opted for showmanship. Five antique cars were dragged into the entrance hall of the house and put on show. Outside, he staged the first country-house jazz festival.

'A colourful **man-about-town,** Lord Montagu
enjoyed **old cars, jazz** and
high living. Above all, he loved Beaulieu ...'

Lord Montagu's Beaulieu (pronounced Bewley) was criticized by his contemporaries but widely imitated. The adjacent National Motor Museum has never looked back. The house has been made part of the same experience. Here the English aristocrat is impresario and his family an exhibit. Hardly a caption in the guide is not in the first person singular. In his portrait by John Ward, Lord Montagu includes his two wives together with his children, horse, dogs and a 1909 Rolls-Royce Silver Ghost. Beaulieu is a rejoinder to all who find stately homes bloodless and impersonal.

The Abbey lies on a bend in the tidal Beaulieu River. The view from the south is idyllic. The site is that of a Cistercian abbey, of which the cloisters and dormitory remain. These have been carefully restored and converted as part of the museum. Palace House itself was the abbey gatehouse, where guests would be greeted and entertained. It contained a porch, hall and two first-floor chapels, and was converted into a manor house by the Wriothesleys, Earls of Southampton, after the Dissolution.

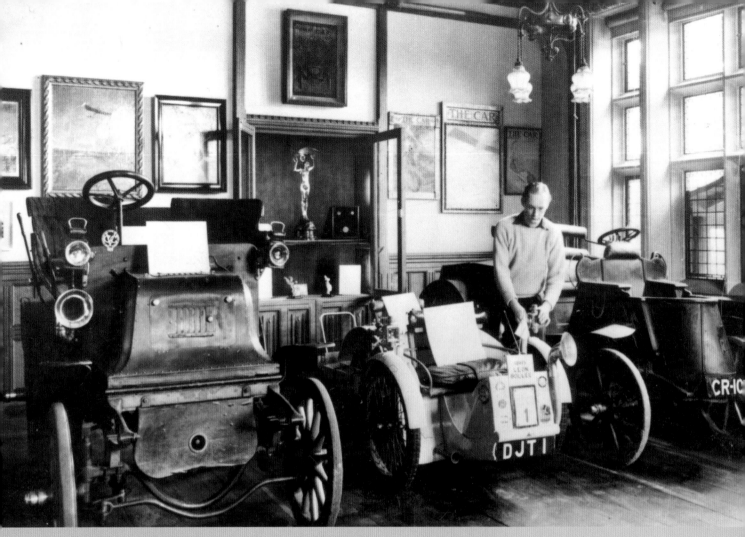

Above When Lord Montagu opened Beaulieu to the public in 1952 he had five veteran cars put on show in the entrance hall of Palace House, and the car museum was born. It was in part a tribute to his father. The first car appeared on England's roads in 1894 and within 10 years motoring was so popular some regulation was needed. John Douglas-Scott-Montagu was an early champion of the motor car and spoke in its favour in Parliament.

The house passed by marriage to the Dukes of Buccleuch in the 19th century and thus to the present baron's great-grandfather. It was extensively rebuilt by the Gothic revivalist, Sir Arthur Blomfield. While he retained what he could of the medieval work, the house is mostly Victorian, colourful and busy. Montagus, old and young, are everywhere. Although they live in rooms upstairs, there is no sense of this being anything but a family home.

The entrance hall contains modern portraits and a Wilton carpet designed by Lord Montagu's son, Ralph, based on an Abbey tile pattern. The original 14th-century inner hall survives as a dining room, and includes information on how medieval meals were eaten. It has a stone ribbed vault, as does the adjacent lower drawing room. This contains a large travelling medicine chest, which was used by the present Lord Montagu's asthmatic grandfather. The kitchen has been re-created in its Victorian form.

Upstairs are two former chapels, now an ante-room and an upper drawing room, where the ladies of the house would gather. The drawing room is prettily decorated with Gothick stencils, cusped tracery in its windows and a wooden beamed roof. The dining room has linenfold panelling salvaged from the old House of Commons. The guide is meticulous in describing how each of these rooms has been used by Montagus past and present.

Bishop's Waltham palace

At Bishop's Waltham, 8 miles E of Southampton; English Heritage, open part year

The palace was reputedly the finest of the many residences of the Bishops of Winchester, outshining Wolvesey (now ruined) and Farnham Castle (Surrey). It was built by King Stephen's brother, Henry of Blois, in the 12th century and rebuilt by William of Wykeham in the late 14th. It ranked in splendour with his work at Winchester and New College, Oxford. William is known to have used his master mason, William de Wynford, at Waltham, as well as Henry Yevele and Hugh Herland, bringing together the work of the three great names of English late-Gothic architecture.

Their work embraced a new hall, tower chambers and service buildings. All survive to full height but in ruined form. The shattered windows of the outer wall indicate the scale of the work. Wykeham's successor, Cardinal Beaufort, half-brother of Henry IV, expanded and added further storeys. Here he entertained Henry VI's queen, Margaret, during the Wars of the Roses. She lay in Beaufort's 'blue bed of gold and damask ... and three suits of the arras hangings', all of which he bequeathed to her in his will. Queen Mary I also stayed here as she eagerly awaited the arrival of her husband, Philip of Spain.

The palace did not survive the Civil War, having been garrisoned by Royalists troops. The bishops concentrated their subsequent building work closer to Winchester. It is now a quiet but atmospheric spot.

Breamore house

Near Breamore, 7 miles S of Salisbury; private house, open part year

Mention the Renaissance to most country gentry of the Elizabethan period and I am sure they would have muttered against all that foreign nonsense. What was good enough for the Middle Ages was good enough for them. They preferred plain building, brick without ornament, with deep gables, tall chimneys and stone-mullioned windows.

The Breamore estate was bought by William Dodington in the 1570s and a new house completed in 1583. Dodington later committed suicide while awaiting 'a suit pending in Star Chamber', not the first to suffer that fate. His house passed by marriage to the Grevilles of Warwick Castle. In 1748, they sold it to Sir Edward Hulse whose family occupy it to this day. It remains a working rural estate, gracious and uncommercialized.

The house's façade is a conservative E-plan, its main rooms looking over the valley of the Hampshire Avon to the New Forest. The pink-red brickwork is aged with lichen and lime. The interior is late Elizabethan, much battered in a Victorian fire but well restored. The entrance is to the rear through what is now an inner hall.

The Great Hall is beyond, looking out over the view. It is a sumptuous room with geometrical plasterwork and two Mannerist chimneypieces, coated in chunky pilasters, grotesques and heraldic cartouches. The panelled walls have tapestries and paintings, including a Gheeraerts of Sir Thomas Coningsby with his dwarf. Here too is a Teniers, *The Coming Storm*, which I saw as just such a storm was gathering outside. I could imagine the same party of peasants racing for cover in Breamore yard.

The dining room contains four still-lifes by Peter Rysbrack, father of the sculptor. The Blue Drawing Room is more feminine, with white walls and 18th-century furniture, including a lovely Chinese Chippendale mirror over the fireplace. In the West Drawing Room is an early

Below The Great Hall at Breamore is some 84 feet long and 21 feet wide (25.5 by 6.5m). The works of art lining its walls include a portrait of Charles I's children by Van Dyck and two Brussels tapestries, dating from around 1630, by David Teniers that show rustic scenes of fishing and harvesting.

cricketing picture, *The Boy with the Bat*, of *c*1760. A rare early English carpet of 1614, covered in exquisite arabesques and foliage, hangs over the staircase.

On the staircase landing is a remarkable ethnographical treasure, a set of 14 *casta* paintings celebrating the intermarriage of different races in Mexico and the New World. They were painted, *c*1720, by Juan Rodriguez Juarez and are believed to be the only complete set in England. Next to them hangs an Indian feather fan. These works were all captured from a Spanish galleon by one of Charles I's privateers, Admiral Westrow, who gave them to his niece, wife of Edward Hulse. They lend an exotic touch to very English Breamore.

The bedrooms, restored after the Victorian fire, are furnished with four-posters, tapestries and precious hangings. In the Blue Bedroom is a set of pastels of the Hulse family by Francis Cotes, as vivid in colour as any oil. Each window has a view over the lovely Hampshire landscape. There is no formal garden at Breamore, just woods and fields, calm and serene.

Bucklers Hard

Near Beaulieu, 9 miles S of Southampton; museum, open all year

Buckler's Hard is a hamlet that grew up round an 18th-century boat-building yard on the Beaulieu River. Despite being partly a museum, the houses are all occupied and shops, school, chapel and pub are still active. There are, however, no cars and no television aerials. The river front remains navigable; it was from here that Sir Francis Chichester set sail round the world in 1966.

The houses were the beginnings of a model town intended by the 2nd Duke of Montagu in the 1720s. The ambitious project collapsed after a failed venture in America. The settlement remained a centre of shipbuilding and now yachting. The paved street was replaced by a gravel drive in 1971. The enterprise is now part of the Beaulieu Estate, to whom we owe the taste with which it has been restored. Various houses come under the auspices of the Maritime Museum. The designers have sought authenticity in everything, but those averse to waxwork should stay away.

Labourer's cottage *

At the start Buckler's Hard had neither church nor school and most goods had to be fetched on foot from Beaulieu. The gulf between a skilled worker, as at the Shipwright's Cottage (right), and a mere labourer was a yawning one. This is a house of utter poverty, just one bay wide. It is displayed more or less as acquired by the museum, with the most rudimentary furnishings restored in a late 18th-century setting. So cramped are the two rooms, one up, one down plus a tiny kitchen, that it can only be seen through holes cut in the wall of the adjacent house.

The characters depicted, James and Elizabeth Bound with their four children, lived in the house in the 18th century. The guidebook points out that others in the village might have been even poorer. This family at least had regular protein and vegetables in their diet.

Upstairs is a single bedroom with a small fireplace but no beds. On the floor are two mattresses, one for the adults and one for the children. How six people fitted in here is a mystery. A mouse eats the cheese in the kitchen.

New inn *

The first building at the top of the street is a house and shop that became the New Inn in 1792. It has been reconstructed as it might have been in the evening, with known historical characters from the village portrayed in effigy, drinking and chatting. Even their conversation is re-created through recordings. An elderly shipwright plays cards on a settle. Joseph Wort, the landlord, is at the bar in conversation. His daughter examines the wares of a travelling tinker while the local blacksmith does a deal with a visiting iron merchant.

The re-creation is vivid, portraying not just the building and decoration but clothes and everyday objects more naturally than on hangers or in cases. Anecdote is brought to life. Above all sound is welcome, a dimension absent from most English historic buildings; here it is in the form of a careful Hampshire dialect. This is an admirable tableau of working-class life.

Shipwright's cottage *

Here is a reinstatement of the cottage of a more prosperous worker, Thomas Burlace, who lived here from 1789 to 1820. It comprises a sitting room, an alcove for storing apples and a small rear kitchen. In the latter, we see Burlace coming home after work, his precious adze over his arm. Apart from the food in the kitchen, a quantity of laundry indicates the family's comparative wealth.

Burlace's wife and daughter are in the living room; Mrs Burlace is working on a rag rug. Upstairs in the bedroom another daughter looks after her baby sister. A further bedroom is on the second floor. I find the place just too spotless for comfort. Did these people really find time to scrub and whitewash their abode every week?

Above Thomas Burlace could have earned as much as £70 a year as a shipwright. With an annual rent of £4, this left the family enough surplus income to afford a servant to help Arabella Burlace with the housework. This freed their daughters from some of the domestic chores and gave Arabella time to make rugs and other linens for her home and family.

Chawton:
Jane Austen's house

Genteel home of the great author during the last years of her life

At Chawton, 1 mile SW of Alton; museum, open all year

Austen lived at Chawton for the last seven years of her life, from 1809 to 1817. It saw her last masterpieces, *Mansfield Park* and *Emma*. The house had been inherited by one of her many brothers and was furnished by him for his widowed mother and sisters. They lived happily but always in straitened circumstances. After their deaths, the house became farm cottages until it was acquired by the Jane Austen Trust and opened as a museum in 1949.

Austen's work cannot be commemorated in inanimate objects. The custodians have been able to do little beyond creating a 'Jane lived here' museum. The drawing room has no armchairs and the bedrooms no beds. The collection is of Georgian antiques and Austen memorabilia, with no suggestion of the busyness or clutter with which the family must have been surrounded. The most human touch is the still-squeaking door, kept that way so Jane would have time to clear away her writing materials should visitors approach.

That said, much is instructive. The drawing room contains the piano to which the Austen girls loved to dance and a Hepplewhite bureau belonging to their father. There are two topaz crosses, the booty which Jane's sailor brother, Charles, brought back from the Napoleonic wars. In the dining parlour is the table where Jane used to serve meals and settle down to write after breakfast.

The upstairs rooms are laid out as a museum, mostly with pictures and documents on the walls. In the bedroom which Jane shared with her

This house might have sprung from a Jane Austen novel. The old building in friendly redbrick sits in the village centre where the old Alton–Winchester road turns a corner. Behind its rose-clad windows and wicket fence, a novelist might watch the world pass by and commit it to her notebook. The house is comfortable without ostentation, genteel but not rich. Here an Austen heroine could dream of launching herself into social orbit, yet safely retreat should she fall.

'Here an Austen heroine could dream ...'

Jane Austen
1775–1817

Jane Austen was born in the rectory of Steventon in Hampshire on 16th December 1775. When her father retired in 1801, the Austens moved to Bath. In 1809, Jane, her sister and now-widowed mother moved to Chawton. By late 1816 Jane was gravely ill. The following May she moved to Winchester to be nearer her doctor. She died there on 18th July 1817 and was buried in the cathedral.

Above Jane's brother Edward, who owned Chawton, had a new Regency-style window put into the drawing room to overlook the garden and blocked up the window that overlooked the road to give his mother and sisters greater privacy.

beloved sister, Cassandra, are examples of her needlework. The Admirals' Room reflects the family's links with the sea, two brothers serving in Nelson's navy. Exhibits include an exotic bell brought back by Charles from the siege of Rangoon. At the end of the passage is a small display of Georgian ladies' costumes. To them could surely be added stills from the many period dramas inspired by the novels.

The garden is smaller than in Jane's day but still boasts the flowers that fill her books – pinks, sweet williams, columbines and peonies. The donkey cart in which she visited local friends is in the barn.

Elvetham hall

★★ Supreme example of Victorian Gothic-style architecture

Near Hartley Wintney, 8 miles E of Basingstoke; now a hotel

The Elvetham, they call it now. If a modern conference hotel and 'advanced learning environment' is the only way to save desperate Victorian mansions, so be it. Elvetham has been transformed from wreck to splendour. Little has been altered beyond the chapel (now a squash court) and much has been revived. Twenty years ago it faced demolition.

The house is a rare domestic work of the Victorian Gothicist, S. S. Teulon. The estate had belonged to Seymours in the Tudor period and reputedly saw an evening's revelry attended by Elizabeth I, on which legend has it Shakespeare based (vaguely) *A Midsummer Night's Dream.* The oak she planted is still here.

The old house passed by marriage into the Gough family, Barons Calthorpe, and was rebuilt by Teulon for the 4th Baron in 1859. It was sold to ICI in 1953, passing through various hands until acquired and restored in its present form in 2001. The estate is still owned by the Calthorpes.

Calthorpe's building survives virtually intact. He wanted Teulon to conjure into life the antique works he had admired on his European travels, as had the Grand Tourists of old. His tour had been conducted in the company of Victoria's eldest son, the Prince of Wales. Hence the works were not of Greece and Rome but of Gothic Northern Europe. Teulon, lover of medieval polychromy, was the man to re-create them.

The exterior is (still) hard to find beautiful. The red-and-black banded and diapered brickwork is harsh on the eye. Dark turrets and towers seem grotesque in this peaceful setting. It is what Mark Girouard calls Teulon's 'belligerent chaos'.

The interiors are of a piece. The theme of medieval chivalry runs from the entrance hall through to the staircase hall and the reception rooms. Everywhere are panelled ceilings painted with medieval motifs. The drawing room illustrates Walter Scott's *Kenilworth*, cult mid-Victorian novel. The stained glass carries scenes

Left A massive stained-glass window illuminates the main staircase. The ceiling above is decorated with signs of the Zodiac, and representations of Night, Day and the Four Seasons. **Below** Among the panels of decorative glass in the main hall is this equestrian portrait of Robert the Bruce, King of Scotland. The window is set above a fireplace designed by Teulon, Elvetham Hall's architect, to look like an altar – the chimney flue is concealed in the window frame.

Right In 1591, Elizabeth I and a retinue of 500 visited the Earl of Hertford, then owner of Elvetham. A 19th-century stone mason re-created the moment of her arrival for the frieze above the drawing-room fireplace.

from Arthurian legends, Elizabethan romances and local Hampshire history. The whole forms a remarkable artistic programme.

The best features of the rooms are the fireplaces. Some are decorative beyond description. Gone are the classical myths and heraldic boasts of the classicists and neo-Jacobeans. Here tales are told of noble deeds in stone and paintwork. The drawing room fireplace has Queen Elizabeth arriving at the house. The dining room portrays Raleigh and Essex declaiming to the public, either from the pulpit or the dock.

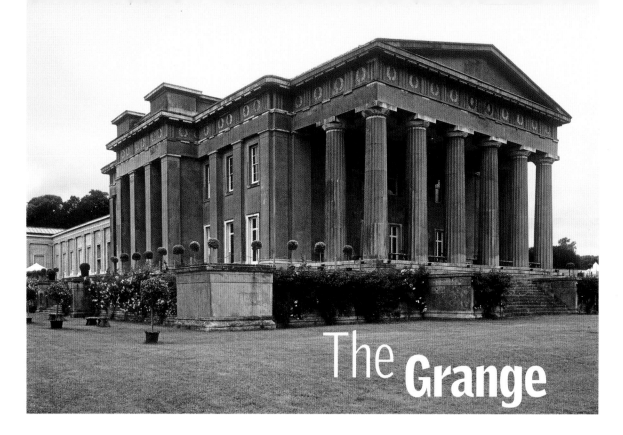

The Grange

★ ★ Ruin of early Greek-revival mansion, now the setting for opera performances

Near Northington, 6 miles NE of Winchester; English Heritage, open all year

I first saw this house wholly derelict. The Barings, owners of the neighbouring Stratton estate, were intending to dynamite it. They had already destroyed George Dance's Stratton Park across the lake and Norman Shaw's Baring's Bank building in the City of London. At The Grange, magnificent plaster ceilings were falling to the floor and the central roof was on the point of collapse. The place had been maltreated by American soldiers billeted here during the Second World War, but was not yet a ruin. Within a few years of my visit, it was a total loss.

The Grange has now been stabilized by English Heritage and given a roof, but that organization's scorched earth policy of restoration resulted in all the interiors being lost. Since then an opera house has been added as a succubus, tucked into the side of the hill and penetrating the rear wall of the building.

The Grange is important both historically and scenically. The architect, C. R. Cockerell, who embellished the building in the 1820s, declared that it was as good as Poussin. The house was one of the early Greek revival set pieces in Georgian England (with Hammerwood Park, West Sussex, and Belsay Castle, Northumberland). It was designed in 1804 by William Wilkins who encased an earlier 17th-century house for the Barings' predecessors, the Drummonds. Wilkins was already engaged in the battle of 'Romans versus Greeks' at Downing College, Cambridge, which he won for the Greeks. At The Grange he erected a copy of the Athens Theseion. Eight columns of mighty solidity gaze from the portico over a sweep of parkland to the lake.

The house cannot have seemed a friendly place. The sides have severe pilastered walls. The whole thing is largely for show, not of stone but of cement render over brick. Yet the interiors were sumptuous, some surviving from the 17th century but the hall reconstructed by Wilkins. Cockerell's conservatory has been rebuilt and the whole place thoroughly tidied up for opera-goers.

If The Grange must be a ruin, I preferred it left, like the trunk of Ozymandias, splendid and decayed amid the rooks, cedars and memories. Now it is a stage set.

Highclere castle

✭ ✭ ✭ Grand Victorian mansion by architect Sir Charles Barry

Near Highclere, 5 miles S of Newbury; private house, open part year

Highclere is the only house I know where the client constantly protested that the architect was not spending enough money. In 1838, Sir Charles Barry was asked for a new house by the 3rd Earl of Carnarvon, junior line of the Herberts of Wilton. Barry's proposals were twice rejected as too modest and he and Carnarvon spent their lives in ceaseless argument. Carnarvon queried every detail, usually for its lack of ostentation. He also disliked the existing Capability Brown landscape, which he Victorianized with conifers, rhododendrons and follies. Highclere emerged as the archetypal early-Victorian mansion, although it was not completed until the Earl and Barry were both dead.

Highclere's most celebrated occupant was his descendant, the 5th Earl, who financed and led Howard Carter's Tutankhamun expedition, during which he died in Egypt, whether of blood poisoning or of the notorious curse nobody knows. The present Earl, who lives elsewhere on the estate, is racing manager to the Queen. The guidebook depicts the house like a

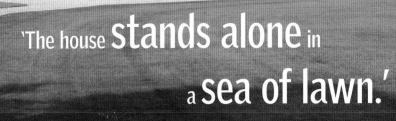

'The house **stands alone** in a **sea of lawn**.'

Right The floor in the entrance hall, by William Butterfield, features two interlocking 'C's that stand for 'Comes Carnarvon'. The same cypher can be seen among the ceiling bosses. Centre right The entrance hall opens into the Saloon, designed by Thomas Allom. The lower walls are covered with leather panels, dated to 1631, that were brought back from Cordoba in Spain by the 3rd Earl and hung here in 1862. Far right The oak staircase rises up through Highclere's tower. It took nearly a year to carve and install.

shimmering wedding cake, framed by a great cedar and with three horses being led past as if to the start of a race.

The house stands alone in a sea of lawn. Barry did not demolish the Georgian house but encased its brick walls in stone, festooning the roofs with Elizabethan strapwork and finials. A large tower was added, reminiscent of his Victoria Tower at the Palace of Westminster. The porch is guarded by two armorial wyverns. The house is thus more a work of embellishment than original architecture, but its decorative impact is tremendous.

By the time the walls were finished, the 4th Earl had turned to Thomas Allom and others for the interiors. The result is a series of eclectic but sumptuous rooms. The entrance hall is said to be by Sir Gilbert Scott and might be the transept of a church. Its polychrome floor is by the master of Gothic colour, William Butterfield. Beyond is the Saloon, the heart of the house, a baronial hall rising to the roof. This is Arthurian Gothic. The space is top-lit with a balcony above heraldic panels of Herberts and Carnarvons. The lower walls are covered in tooled and gilded leather from Cordoba.

From the rooms of bishops and barons, one passes to those that might be a comfortable Pall Mall club. The library, probably by Allom, is like Barry's Reform Club, full of male opulence and the motifs of a Grecian gymnasium. The ceiling is panelled and gilded, the bookshelves likewise. The fireplace surrounds are after Grinling Gibbons.

The adjacent music room and drawing room offer a contrast, redecorated in French 18th-century style by Almina, wife of the 5th Earl and a Rothschild relation. In the drawing room are family portraits by Reynolds and Beechey,

notably of children. The smoking room has a magnificent Jan Weenix still-life over the fireplace and works by Van Goyen and Wouwerman. Hidden in a space between the two rooms, a collection of Egyptian archaeological treasures was found in 1987. The 5th Earl's entire collection had supposedly been sold to New York's Metropolitan Museum in 1923 but these items had clearly been forgotten (or hidden). The surviving items are now displayed in the basement.

Highclere never takes itself too seriously. The elephantine staircase behind the hall is lightened by a sentimental Italian statue of Carnarvon children and a Reynolds of Mrs Musters as Hebe. Wherever a bit of wall is spare, someone has crammed in a Roman trophy or a heroic portrait. The downstairs dining room is a gallery of such pictures, mostly of Stuart cavaliers.

Lord Carnarvon
1866–1923

After a series of accidents that damaged his lungs, George Herbert, 5th Earl of Carnarvon, was advised to spend the winter in warmer climes. He went to stay at the Winter Palace Hotel in Luxor on the Nile, and so began his fascination with Egyptology. He started funding Howard Carter in 1907 and in 1915 won the concession to dig in the Valley of the Kings. It was there, in November 1922, that Carter discovered Tutankhamun's tomb. Sadly, the Earl died of septicemia soon after; at the moment of his death, back home at Highclere, his favourite dog also died.

Hinton Ampner

☆☆ Re-creation of a neo-Georgian masterpiece

At Hinton Ampner, 8 miles E of Winchester; National Trust, open part year

In 1960 Hinter Ampner was gutted by fire. The creation of the neo-classical antiquarian, Ralph Dutton, the house was totally destroyed, along with his collection of furniture, pictures and books. So intense was the heat that antique volumes in the library calcified in their bookcases and had to be chipped out with pickaxes. Dutton seemed rejuvenated by the catastrophe. Rather than abandon the place, he set about building a new house and amassing a new collection. The present structure is essentially a monument to his determination. The renaissance is as related in his account of the work, *A Hampshire Manor*.

Hinton had been a Dutton house since its heiress married the 2nd Lord Sherborne in 1820. It was rebuilt after 1864 in a Tudor style described by Ralph Dutton in 1936 as of 'exceptional hideousness'. Ralph promptly remodelled it, reverting to the then fashionable neo-Georgian. What he was to reconstruct after the fire could thus be said to merit the term, neo-neo-Georgian.

The outcome was regarded by another antiquarian, Sir Brinsley Ford, as 'the most beautiful neo-Georgian interior in England'. Dutton, who became the last Lord Sherborne in 1982, died in 1985 and left the house and garden to the National Trust.

The exterior is uninteresting, a conventional box of suburban 18th-century revival. The inside is more dramatic. Dutton transformed the old Tudor entrance hall from dark oak and sporting trophies into an aesthete's stage-set of marble floor, scagliola columns, giltwood and Louis XVI furniture. The other rooms he likewise Georgianized, the work illustrated in before-and-after photographs in the guidebook. The furniture is predominantly French, the pictures Italian. In the drawing room, the mirrors have extravagant Rococo frames. An exquisite clock is of French porcelain. A no less exquisite carpet is *c*1800 from 'the collection of the Princess de Broglie, Paris'.

Echoes of Robert Adam survive in some of the rooms. Dutton made casts of ceilings and rescued fireplaces from Adam houses being demolished between the wars in London's Adelphi and Berkeley Square. The ceiling in the dining room was re-created after the fire, its Angelica Kauffmann roundels replaced by Elizabeth Biddulph.

The garden is spread along the line of hills south of Alresford. Everything about the approach is immaculate, embracing farm buildings and church. Beyond are terraces and walks leading to dells and rose gardens. Dutton remarked that 'what above all I want from a garden is tranquillity'. I fear that is the one quality that popular Hinton Ampner may now have to go without.

Below The plasterwork ceiling in the dining room was originally created for 38 Berkeley Square, a London town house designed by Robert Adam. It was rescued in 1940 and given a new home at Hinton Ampner. Half the ceiling was destroyed in the 1960 fire and has since been reconstructed.

Houghton lodge

⋆ ⋆ *Cottage orné*, originally built as a fishing lodge, on the bank of the River Test

Near Houghton, 8 miles S of Andover; private house, open by appointment, gardens open part year

The idyllic *cottage orné* of Houghton crowns a hillock on a bend in the River Test. It is the perfect embodiment of Georgian Picturesque. In such houses, wrote Mark Girouard, 'jaded noblemen or well-heeled city merchants could retire with a mere handful of servants to taste the delights of rustic simplicity'. In the town, their mansions created an illusion of grandeur. In the country their cottages were illusions of poverty, like Marie Antoinette on her farm.

Houghton Lodge is one of the best examples of *cottage orné* architecture. The house is open by appointment, but can be perambulated and appreciated from outside. It is approached from the

Above The typical *cottage orné* offered its Georgian visitors a rural retreat and the chance to sample some of the pleasures of the countryside – Houghton was probably built as a fishing lodge. The interior decoration reflects the Gothick style of the architecture, so popular with the Picturesque movement of the late 18th and early 19th centuries.

stables adjoining an impressive walled garden. The walls are of a rare chalk-cob construction, chalk and straw mixed and laid layer on layer as each dried. Greenhouses contain exotic orchids, jasmine and plumbago in profusion. Beneath it is a spectacular herbaceous border.

The main lawn spreads between the walled garden and the River Test as a green plinth to the Lodge above. Built around 1800, it has four Gothick bays to the south and a bow window and iron veranda to the east, under a conical roof. The main roof is steep, with deep bargeboarded dormers and high neo-Tudor chimneys, bundled together as if in fear of toppling. The roof would once have been thatched but is now tiled and shingled, a solecism that might one day be corrected.

Hurst castle

★ Henrician coastal fortress, with defences extended in the 19th century

Near Milford on Sea, 4 miles S of Lymington; English Heritage, open part year

Above The three-storey keep lies at the heart of the Tudor castle. Its ceilings were strengthened c1803 during the Napoleonic Wars, when new guns were placed on the roof. Huge wing batteries (**below**) were added in the 1860s to house 30 heavy guns.

Whatever the weather, Hurst has drama. It stands on a shingle spit jutting out into the Solent and holding the key to its defences. Of all the Henrician coastal forts, this was the most important, recognized by its later refortification. The castle is reached either by ferry from Keyhaven or by walking a mile along the shingle spit.

The original castle was begun in 1541 as a 12-sided tower surrounded by a clover leaf of bastions, bristling with cannon and surrounded by a moat. It was unused in the 17th and 18th centuries, although Charles I was imprisoned here on his way back from the Isle of Wight in 1648. The castle was a prison under the anti-Popery acts, a priest being incarcerated here in 1700 for twenty-nine years until his death. It remained garrisoned and enjoyed a garden and even a fishermen's inn.

The castle was massively extended by the Victorians with two long bat-wing batteries and a lighthouse. Such was its importance that the defences were regularly upgraded to resist each new development of high explosive shells. The fortifications were further strengthened to take big guns in the 20th century. The castle was finally abandoned in the 1950s.

Although the Tudor tower was strengthened and extended and its moat filled, the original interiors survive. The entrance door still has its Tudor arch. The ground floor held the barracks, with more comfortable accommodation for officers on the first floor, with fireplaces and latrines. The walls are of impressive thickness. From the roof is a spectacular view of the Solent and Isle of Wight.

Mottisfont abbey

☆ ☆ A Tudor and Georgian house enclosing the remains of an Augustinian priory

At Mottisfont, 9 miles W of Winchester; National Trust, open part year

Mottisfont is a pleasant walk by wooded streams to a nationally celebrated rose garden. The house exterior is charming, but the interiors are disappointing except for one room. The old Augustinian priory is no more than ghostly fragments starting out of later walls. The Tudor and Georgian house was much abused by the 20th century. The Rex Whistler room, however, must not be missed.

Mottisfont's front and rear façades comprise an architectural textbook. The south front is a mid-Georgian refashioning of what appear to be four separate phases of development. A pedimented redbrick centre is embraced by Tudor stair turrets, then Georgian wings, then further and grander wings, rendered and sitting above terraces. Each seems to be elbowing the other out of the composition. The effect is most enjoyable. The rear is composed of the buttressed wall of the old priory and various fragments of arches, one with waterleaf capitals.

The priory was taken after the Dissolution by the Sandys family and passed by descent to Sir Richard Mills. In 1740 he fashioned the present appearance of the house, including the wings on balustraded terraces. The house decayed gently until, in 1934, it was stripped of all contents and sold to Gilbert Russell and his wife, Maud. Russell was descended, he was delighted to discover, through

Above Rex Whistler's smoking urn in the Gothick-style drawing room he created at Mottisfont. He used *trompe l'œil* effects, rendered in grisaille, to simulate columns, plasterwork and ornamental details.

twenty-six generations from the priory's founder, William Briwere. His wife was a great beauty who sat for Matisse and others.

The Russells redecorated the interior in neo-classical style, similar to that chosen by Ralph Dutton for Hinter Ampner. Its chief interest is the room commissioned in 1938 from Rex Whistler, and painted shortly before the artist died fighting in the Second World War. It is one of his most complete *trompe-l'œil* works, more formal and complex than his mural in the Tent Room at Port Lympne in Kent.

The room is depicted as a Gothick cabinet with quatrefoil tracery and heavy drapes round the windows. Colour is mixed with grisaille. Over the door, Gothick bursts into Rococo swirls. On the right wall is a niche containing a 'smoking urn', surrounded by symbolic objects, a lute, books, a wedding ring and, to one side, a painter's paintbox and brushes. Thus the artist foretold his death.

Portchester
castle

★ Imposing remains of an ancient castle with Roman origins

At Portchester, 2 miles NW of Portsmouth; English Heritage, open all year

Ghosts walk the old quay beneath the walls of Portchester Castle. Here Roman soldiers and colonists arrived in England and made their way into the noisy fort. There is sea on three sides, water lapping over old stones under high ramparts, many with traces of Roman building.

Within is the outer bailey, once a Roman camp and town in its own right, now a vast lawn. In the far corner is the moated inner bailey of the castle proper. This has a keep in one corner, the ruins of Richard II's palace in another and the constable's residence in a third.

The palace celebrated Richard's marriage to the seven-year-old Isabella of France and was a brilliant, compact royal residence. Richard was toppled before it was completed but it was revived as the point of departure of Henry V for France and Agincourt in 1415.

The only building still roofed is the keep. For almost three centuries it was used primarily for prisoners-of-war, Dutch, Spanish and French. The Georgian historian, Edward Gibbon, was briefly governor here and described conditions for the 3,200 prisoners as 'very loathsome and the men's barracks not much better'. The guidebook points out that things cannot have been too bad, since a French prisoner married a local girl in the barracks church. The inmates were allowed to work at shoemaking, and theatrical performances were held upstairs. The keep was closed and fell into ruin after 1819.

All floors are in place and a spectacular view can be had from the roof. There are hidden staircases, grim latrines, murals and graffiti left by prisoners. A dummy prisoner is shown in a hammock on the ground floor and I would have thought English Heritage could include a full complement upstairs, more enthralling than the present display boards and stands.

The place should be given a touch of Bucklers Hard (see page 78).

'Ghosts walk the old quay beneath the walls of Portchester Castle'

Broadlands

★★☆ Palladian house designed by Capability Brown,
now a shrine to Mountbatten

1 mile S of Romsey; private house, undergoing restoration

The house once occupied by Lord Mountbatten shimmers in immaculate yellow-white brick on the banks of the River Test. Like Petworth in Sussex and Knole in Kent, it is aloof from its adjacent town yet still part of it. The house and park were redesigned by Capability Brown for the young 2nd Viscount Palmerston in 1767–9, to house his Grand Tour collection. This involved the diversion of the river to form a sweeping curve near the west front. The house was given a new entrance by Brown's son-in-law, Henry Holland. This is in the form of a dramatic recessed portico.

The exterior of Broadlands is pattern-book Palladian, handsome but rather bloodless. The interior is cool and aristocratic, now very much the home of Mountbatten's grandson, Lord Romsey. A beautifully domed lobby leads into an entrance hall filled with classical sculpture. Both rooms are in soft 'baby blue' with white dressings. On a table in the hall is the *Broadlands Boy on a Dolphin* by Joseph Nollekens, one of the Rome carvers who supplied Grand Tourists with copies when the supply of classical originals was exhausted.

The glory of the house is the work executed by Joseph Rose, Robert Adam's stuccoist, for Brown in 1769. Rose's swirling patterns fill the west front rooms, the drawing room, saloon and Wedgwood Room, lending a welcome gaiety to otherwise formal chambers. Here is a Rose freed from the constraints of Adam's studiously exact notebooks, able to spread his Rococo imagination across the ceilings and, in the saloon, the wall panels as well. So fine are the latter that the room has no space for any pictures. Inset medallions are by Angelica Kauffmann. The view over the lawn to the river is a picture enough.

Apart from its ceiling, the Wedgwood Room was refashioned by Holland, in his (and Wedgwood's) favourite light blue and white. The stucco on the walls is lower in temperature than Rose's work, with room for four Lely portraits. In Holland's dining room is a portrait of Emma Hamilton looking seductive, painted by Sir Thomas Lawrence.

Broadlands seems an improbable shrine to Lord Mountbatten, dashing and slightly raffish *éminence grise* of the Royal Family after the Second World War. He was murdered by the IRA in 1979. An exhibition devoted to him is in the stables, while models of the ships on which he and his father served line the walls of the Ship Passage.

Mountbatten at Broadlands 'out-guns' even Churchill at Chartwell in celebrity photographs. Yet the house is a moving tribute.

'The **view over the lawn** to the **river** is a picture enough.'

King John's house

⭐ Thirteenth-century hall or meeting house with flint and rubble walls and unusual bone floor

Church Street, Romsey; museum, open part year

Mabel Moody sensed that there was something odd about her Victorian cottage. Its thick walls and strangely proportioned windows seemed older than the surrounding tenements. One day in 1927 a workman on the roof disturbed an end wall and discovered the trefoil head of an old window. Mabel hurried round to the local antiquarian, Walter Andrew. With great excitement, he declared that she had discovered Romsey's long-lost hunting lodge, recorded as in use by King John at the turn of the 13th century.

The Moodys of Romsey emerged from the mists of the 18th century as decent tradespeople, cutlers and gunsmiths. They were a backbone of the local economy and society of the sort that house-hunters discover throughout Victorian England. They acquired premises in Church Court opposite the Abbey and soon expanded into the courtyard to the rear.

Yet of nine children born to Charles and Matilda Moody in the late 19th century, just three survived disease and the Great War and none themselves had children. The one boy, William, was a disappointed inventor. Not one of his creations – a lawn edge-cutter, a road sign, safety scissors and a humane poultry killer – succeeded. He wrote a pamphlet on the 'doom' of the British inventor. His sister Mabel inherited the property in Church Court.

Sadly Mabel's cottage was not King John's. The structure within her cottage is now known to have been later, dated to the mid-13th century, possibly a hall or meeting house. It is tall with rubble and flint walls and a substantial chamber on the upper floor. Mabel lived on in the cottage until 1969, when she gave it to the town, and full investigation and restoration began. Adjacent houses were demolished and later walls, partitions and plaster scraped away.

What survives is scant but intriguing. Downstairs is part of a floor made of animal bones, set on end as cobbles and believed to date from its use as a workshop. I have seen this nowhere else.

Upstairs is a fragment of a lovely early Gothic window with dogtooth carving, indicating an important property. Many of the roof beams are original, ring-dated to 1256. A series of graffiti in the old wall plaster include a dog, the head of a man and various heraldic devices. The designs are believed to date to 1306 when Edward I visited Romsey. The theory is that members of his retinue stayed at the house and scratched the graffiti onto the walls with their daggers.

Next door is a Tudor extension, now a teashop, and a delightful Victorian museum devoted to the Moodys.

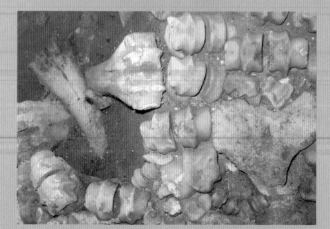

Above There is evidence that a brazier, a worker in bronze, had a workshop at King John's House during the 17th century. The unusual floor, made of bones probably obtained from local tanneries, dates from this time.

Selborne: Gilbert White's house

★★ Home and garden of the famous naturalist

At Selborne, 4 miles SE of Alton; museum, open all year

For millions of English men and women, *The Natural History of Selborne* by Gilbert White (1720–93) has embodied the story of their countryside. The book described the 18th-century landscape of a Hampshire village under a chalk down. It noted the changing seasons and their impact on the flora and fauna. It observed the interdependence of mankind, plants and animals. The book was carried to the ends of empire, reminding imperial generations of the home country and its virtues. White was the English Virgil, celebrant of rural bliss. He was also the first true ecologist, a man who understood nature in the round.

By some miracle, the old house still enjoys the same setting as in White's day. The village

still 'straggles', as he put it, along its one street amid gardens, fields and the slopes of the beech-clad hill, Selborne Hanger. White's own garden is being restored as he created it in the leisure allowed him by his modest duties as local curate. Re-created too are his quaint replicas of landscape ornaments in the style of William Kent.

The house was guarded by enthusiasts for decades after White's death but was put up for sale in the 1950s. After a desperate appeal for funds had failed, the only person who could be found to save it was Robert Oates, who required that a White museum be shared with his kinsman, Captain Oates, who perished on Scott's Antarctic expedition in 1912. This has nothing to

Above White added the Great Parlour to his family home at The Wakes in 1780, to extend the downstairs living area of the house and to afford a view of the garden. Before this addition was built, the main reception room was the Little Parlour, once the hall of the medieval house. Right The curtains and coverlet in his bedroom were embroidered for him by his aunts, who were perhaps mindful of their nephew's interest in nature in choosing floral motifs.

do with Selborne. Indeed it is hard to imagine a more bizarre marriage, of gardening downstairs and Antarctic heroism upstairs. Perhaps gardeners do at least recite Oates's famous last words, 'I am just going outside. I may be some time.'

Gilbert White was just 5 ft 3 ins tall. There is no portrait of him but his effigy stands modestly in the dining room. He never married and devoted his life to the observation and recording of natural phenomena. He was fascinated by interdependence, relating bird migration to harvest and habitat. He wanted every naturalist to dissect a crow each week to examine the contents of its crop. Despite his popularity in his lifetime, he received no scientific recognition.

The core of the house was a medieval hall, The Wakes, which White incorporated into his new dwelling. White added a reception room for a view of his garden and the Downs beyond. It has Georgian furnishings, and family portraits depicting strong, simple English faces. The fire-dogs were for holding hot drinks. In this room, 'Uncle Gilbert' would entertain an array of nephews and nieces with tales of nature.

The hall of the old house became the Little Parlour and contains White's chair, possibly his desk, and various other memorabilia. White's kitchen may have been where he took his meals and where he would continue his observations. Fruit and vegetables would come in from the garden to be inspected and different preservatives tested. The room saw a constant war on cockroaches and house flies. On a shelf lies a desultory Christmas pudding. Upstairs is White's small bedroom. The hangings were stitched for him by his aunts. The table is where he wrote into the night. It is an evocative chamber.

The gardens are as curious as the house. White was clearly eager in his modest way to create a classical landscape in the style of William Kent at Chiswick House (west London). Close to the house are formal topiary, pond garden, herb garden and the 'six quarters' flower beds. A walk leads across the meadow towards the Hanger, including a quincunx of five cypresses arranged as a cross. From here one can see such oddities as a distant statue of Hercules, a barn and White's half-barrel seat in which he would sit and turn gently in the breeze.

'White's small bedroom ... is an evocative chamber.'

Medieval Merchant's house

⭐ Restored house and wine shop with replica medieval furnishings

French Street, Southampton; English Heritage, open part year

Nowhere is the contrast between styles of conservation more glaring than in the two medieval houses in the old part of Southampton. The area was once a lively warren of streets and is now a memorial to England's loss of urban design confidence after the Second World War. While the rest of Europe restored the character of cities such as Warsaw, Hamburg and Tours, the English fled to the suburbs. Inner Southampton is what they left behind, gap-toothed walls, car parks and new buildings erected without thought.

Lost in this wilderness is a fragment of one of England's earliest surviving town houses. The Medieval Merchant's House was erected in about 1290 as house and wine shop. It later became three cottages, a lodging house and a brothel. Bomb-damaged in 1940, it was restored in 1983. The house has been returned to how it appeared in the mid-14th century by the removal of later additions. Only walls, gable timbers and floor members survived and much of this had to be replaced. Medieval furnishings were reproduced from contemporary records. My reaction in that case is why not restore the whole neighbourhood to its ancient form, known from photographs, and give it back some life?

The house plan is unusual. A passage leads past the hall to an inner room at the rear. The hall is open to the roof above while below the floor is earth. There are hangings on the walls and a trestle table. The repointed brick chimney-breast looks like suburban neo-Tudor. The inner room contains a reproduction medieval cupboard. The two upstairs bedchambers are furnished with replicas, the front room with two cosy four-posters. Beneath the house is a brick-floored undercroft where the wine was stored.

The house is a frigid academic exercise, neither a ruin 'as found' nor re-creating the atmosphere of its original. But at least it is still with us and for that we are thankful.

Right The façade of the wine shop has been re-created, complete with wine-barrel sign and wooden shutters that would have doubled as a shop counter. **Left** The hall at the Merchant's House has been furnished with replica pieces, copied either from medieval manuscripts or surviving examples of contemporary furniture.

Above Next to the museum, garden designer Sylvia Landsberg has re-created a Tudor garden using suitable period plantings with an emphasis on culinary and medicinal herbs, such as lavender and parsley.

Tudor house

★★ The imposing medieval town house of a wealthy customs official

Bugle Street, Southampton; museum, undergoing restoration

The house dates from the 15th century and is the best surviving medieval building in Southampton. It was the property of a wealthy citizen, Sir John Dawtrey, Controller of Customs. His widow Isobel was a merchant in her own right, dealing in building stone. She is one of the few ladies of the period of whose appearance we have a record, for she later married a Lord Chief Justice and was painted by Holbein.

The house is of close-studded timbering and wide windows. It was restored in 1895 and became a local museum in 1912. Since then, each generation of curators felt obliged to add his or her mark, in signs, captions, notices, warnings and educational diktats. While the Medieval Merchant's House (left) is a private conversation between archaeologists, the Tudor House is a municipal memorandum. It remains to be seen how much of this administrative clutter is reinstated after the current restoration.

Behind the bureaucracy is a fine Tudor building. Its core is a lofty hall, left in its much-altered 19th-century state, with a large Gothic window and fireplace. The screens passage and gallery appear original. A door leads into a small rear garden, delightfully re-created in Tudor style. Crammed into its tiny space are arbours, knots, squares, herb beds and even an orchard. Tudor posts carrying heraldic emblems have been erected. An old cannon points appropriately at an ugly modern hotel opposite. It should be regularly fired.

Future exhibits are still to be decided. On my visit, a small writing room upstairs, properly furnished, led into the Baltic room. Here were a chest and chair, inlaid with ivory. The remaining rooms were a museum. A Georgian attic extension was filled with so much real junk as to defeat all curatorial discipline. It included a magnificent pennyfarthing.

Stratfield Saye house

The Duke of Marlborough was given Blenheim. Winston Churchill bought Chartwell. The Duke of Wellington found himself somewhere in between. As his prize for victory, he chose a comfortable Carolean mansion near Basingstoke, largely for the quality of the land. He considered Uppark, in Sussex, and even pondered building a palace across the River Loddon from Stratfield Saye, for which a number of architects submitted schemes. But the cost and an affection for the old house left him content. He had grandeur to spare in his London home, Apsley House. The Duke's descendants live in the house to this day.

From the outside, Stratfield Saye looks deceptively domestic. Indeed, its modesty was treated with derision by Wellington's contemporaries. The house is long and low, two storeys with dormers in the roof and Dutch gables on the wings. Painted white, it might be in Cape Town. Its builder, probably in 1635, was an early member of the Pitt dynasty. The central portion of the garden front was inserted by a later Pitt in 1740. This portion looks like a totally different mansion forcing itself to the centre of the composition like a creature from a different age.

The interior was much altered by a later Pitt, Lord Rivers, in the mid-18th century and has a stateliness lacking in the exterior. The hall rises two storeys, with a gallery over marbled wooden columns. Paintings are of battle scenes and portraits of all the Wellingtons from the lst Duke to the present day. Into the floor are set mosaics from the Roman town at neighbouring Silchester. Its loss is Stratfield Saye's gain.

The library is sumptuous, in the manner of William Kent. Gilded rosettes fill the ceiling and gilded foliage the cornice. The walls are lined with leather books, some of them Napoleon's.

Everywhere are Wellington memorabilia. There is a lock of George Washington's hair and another of the hair of the Duke's horse, Copenhagen. This noble mount is buried in the grounds and has the entire music room as its shrine. The staircase is from the early house, heavy and friendly.

Lady Douro's Room commemorates Augusta Pierrepont, who married the Great Duke's second son and heir. Those who find Wellington names confusing (Wellesley, Douro, Mornington) should not attempt the Pierreponts, who embrace Kingstons, Manvers, Medows, Cecils and Exeters. Instead, enjoy a delightful set of family portraits and a Rococo fireplace.

The print room and gallery are decorated with contemporary prints as wallpaper, a brief fashion of the 18th century and rarely in such profusion as at Stratfield Saye. The print room also has whimsical Rococo designs in the ceiling. The gallery is more majestic, its prints offset by classical busts in partly gilded bronze. France appears to have won in style what it lost in battle. The Duke spent freely in Paris to furnish both his houses.

Both the small and large drawing rooms have bright French wallpaper and Rococo decoration. In the former is a charming painting of the Great Duke in old age, surrounded by his offspring. The rooms contain pictures captured after the Battle of Vitoria during the Peninsular campaign. Like those at Apsley House, many had been stolen by the French from the Spanish royal collection and were granted to Wellington as a present by the Spanish king. Some had been used to protect pack horses from the rain. They survived remarkably well.

The grounds contain a magnificent stand of Wellingtonias, sequoias first named in honour of the Duke when they arrived in England in 1853.

The Vyne

★★★★ Tudor house with 18th-century classical and Gothick interiors

At Sherborne St John, 4 miles N of Basingstoke; National Trust, open part year

The Vyne is the classic house of the English gentleman down the best of ages. Its style embraces Tudor, early Palladian, Georgian Gothick and Victorian revival. It is a model of steady stylistic accretion and the loveliest mansion in Hampshire.

The first part of the building was erected 1518–27 by William Sandys, Lord Chamberlain to Henry VIII. It was acquired in 1653 by Chaloner Chute, Speaker of the Cromwellian House of Commons. He commissioned Inigo Jones's pupil, John Webb, to classicize the façade. A century later his descendant, John Chute, came back from the Grand Tour and produced a bravura set of classical and Gothick interiors. The house then mercifully went to sleep. Later Chutes dusted its eyelids and tucked in its sheets, until they handed it to the National Trust in good order in 1956.

'... the loveliest mansion in Hampshire.'

A walk round the exterior reveals Webb's portico of the mid-1650s, said to be the first on an English country house. To the west is a long range with the 16th-century Oak Gallery above. Entry is through the Stone Gallery, created below the Oak Gallery and filled with John Chute's Grand Tour acquisitions. A small corner room served as a classroom during The Vyne's brief time as a school in the early 20th century. It is now hung with silk. I would have preferred it left as a schoolroom.

The rooms along the portico front were mostly restored to their 17th-century appearance by a Victorian descendant, the antiquary Wiggett Chute. The drawing room has a light-hearted Rococo ceiling but faded wall-hangings and dark pictures. Beyond the vestibule is a saloon, again with dark panelling and pictures hung in tiers round a piano and harp. For the parlour, Wiggett Chute brought Tudor linenfold panels from elsewhere in the house. The restoration of these wonderfully atmospheric rooms was aided by Martha Chute's watercolours of the 1860s.

The ante-chapel and chapel date from the Tudor house but received the attention of John Chute from 1755. Here 18th-century Gothick overlays Tudor. The ante-room was fashioned from the nave of the old chapel, with lozenge fretwork panels. The chapel is of extraordinary richness; its gallery

Left The Oak Gallery is a remarkable survivor from the early 16th century. The panelling would have been installed by the original owner, William Sandys, in around 1521. Carvings of the insignia of some of the most powerful Tudor families were worked into the linenfold design. **Below left** The decor in the Print Room dates from 1804. Many of the original prints deteriorated badly over the years and by 1959 had mostly been replaced with the examples now on display. **Right** John Chute created the staircase and hall between 1769 and 1771. Roman emperors Caligula and Antoninus – in mid-18th-century Italian marble representations – regard visitors from the newel posts as they begin the ascent to the magnificent upper landing. **Below** The royal coat of arms, flanked by the Sandys crest, is mounted above a doorway in the Oak Gallery, recalling William Sandys' position as Henry VIII's Lord Chamberlain.

dates from Lord Sandys' time, as do the Tudor choir stalls. Most remarkable is Chute's *trompe-l'œil* Gothick vaulting of the gallery, apparently a Horace Walpole suggestion. The murals were executed in 1769 by the splendidly named artist, Spiridione Roma.

The glass in the chapel is from the best Flemish work of the early 16th century, the classical enrichment of the upper and lower lights being particularly fine. So too is the glass in the eerie Tomb Chamber next door. This was designed by John Chute himself as monument to his 17th-century ancestor, Speaker Chute. The effigy lies recumbent on a chest adorned with coats of arms and swags.

The Vyne's masterpiece is the central staircase and landing that John Chute created in place of the old Great Hall of the house. He sketched Gothick, chinoiserie and classical designs but the choice fell on classical. The stairs thus rise symmetrically through three planes to an upper landing, each volume carefully modulated. The coffered ceilings and

Above The *trompe l'œil* murals in the Chapel, painted by Spiridione Roma in 1769, include representations of the four Gospel writers. On the north wall St Luke is shown with a bull and St Mark with an eagle; the other two evangelists, Matthew and John, are on the south wall.

Left Part of the chapel floor is made up of 16th-century majolica tiles. Originally found in front of the altar, they were re-laid in their current position around the stalls during 19th-century renovations. The tiles are decorated with Flemish interpretations of Italian and classical designs, and were made in Flanders by Italian craftsmen.

fluted columns seem perfectly in scale. Double the proportions and this could be a Russian palace. The colours are not the rich greens and golds of the early Georgians; here all is soft blue and white, Italian serenity. We know of no designer or craftsman other than Chute himself.

Upstairs is the library and a return to Wiggett Chute's neo-Jacobean. Small plaster busts of literary luminaries stand above the bookcases, attended by portraits of 17th-century Chutes. This is a room in which one yearns to pull down a book from these enticing shelves and read. I asked if National Trust members could use these books and was told emphatically not.

Next door are two tapestry rooms, with Indian and chinoiserie designs from the Soho workshops. They lead into the original Sandys Oak Gallery, for once untouched by any Chute hand. This is a rare pre-Elizabethan chamber. Linenfold panels of outstanding quality rise from floor to ceiling, enriched with lavish heraldry of Sandys and other Henrician courtiers. The doorcase is a study in transition, a Gothic opening carrying a royal coat of arms held by cherubs in classical poses.

Compared with the house, The Vyne's grounds are comparatively modest, befitting a Tudor rather than a Palladian mansion. The National Trust has replanted much of the area round the lake and created an Edwardian formal garden near the summer house. This dates from Chaloner Chute's day. The house takes its name from a vine which still grows by the Stone Gallery entrance.

WINCHESTER
The College

WINCHESTER The College

★★ Medieval collegiate complex, set around courtyards

College Street, Winchester; private school, open for tours all year

The college was founded by William of Wykeham in 1382, shortly after his New College at Oxford, and built by his master-mason, William de Wynford. It was for seventy 'poor and needy scholars', and ten commoners who paid fees. The commoners now predominate.

Both colleges were the first in England to be planned as residential academic communities, yet they retained the form of a medieval town house, a walled enclave of gatehouse and utility ranges looking inwards over one or more courtyards. Grand apartments could be kept distinct from lesser ones, but within a joint defensible space.

An aerial view shows a small medieval court reached through a gatehouse from the street, then courts of increasing grandeur beyond. The gatehouse carries a lovely medieval statue of the Virgin in a niche. The outer court was for college services, the bakehouse, brewhouse, laundry, even slaughterhouse. This was the only part of the college into which women were admitted, and then only if they were 'of such an age and appearance as to give rise to no suspicion'. On the far side of the court is a middle gate leading to Chamber Court. This was the core of the medieval college, round which were the rooms of scholars, ushers, chaplains and headmaster.

On the far side of this court is the chapel and hall, back-to-back as at New College. The chapel windows are high and buttressed, its glorious vault covered in red on white Gothick decoration. The hall next door is more domestic, reached by a flight of steps. Below is a range of domestic offices, altered but still evoking the ritual of medieval hospitality. The buttery contains a much-copied painting of the *Trusty Servant* with the ears of an ass, snout of a pig and padlocked jaw. The Treasury contains plate donated to the school over the centuries.

Beyond Chamber Court, Winchester takes on a more institutional character. Cloisters extend round a delightful chantry chapel erected in memory of a college steward, John Fromond. To its right stands 'School', a magnificent Restoration hall and the first room in the college designed specifically for teaching. Legend attributes it to Christopher Wren. On the wall, a board demands '*aut disce*', an admonition either to learn or risk expulsion or a beating.

Left Wykeham dedicated his college to the Virgin Mary; her statue overlooks the outer gatehouse. **Below left** The *Trusty Servant* was painted in 1809 by William Cave to replace a 16th-century wall painting by John Hoskyns. **Below** Most of the stained-glass panels in the Chapel windows are 19th-century copies of medieval originals.

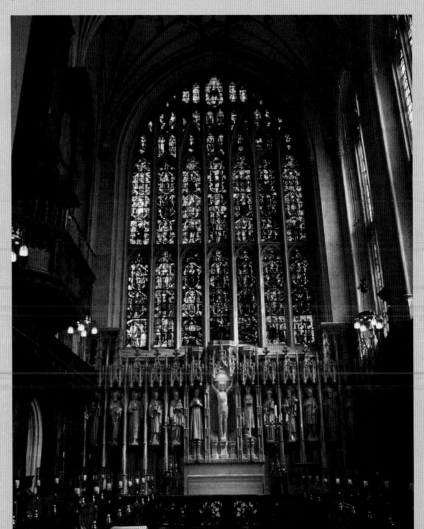

Great hall

★★ Medieval hall, once the Great Hall of Winchester Castle

The Castle, Winchester; museum, open all year

All that remains of the castle that William the Conqueror built and Henry III extended is its Great Hall. But what a hall! It was described in Pevsner as 'the finest medieval hall in England after Westminster Hall'. The palace was for residence as well as ceremony, a place where a king on his progress could show his face to his people, on his own territory and in his own splendour.

The outside setting is Victorian medieval, made bleak by post-war municipal tat. The interior is breathtaking. For much of the 20th century, it served as a local courtroom, but this purpose has been removed and the space restored to its former appearance. The double cube of five giant bays was completed in 1235, with aisles and plate tracery windows. The entrance is Victorian, anachronistically placed in the middle of the façade. The original door was behind a screen at the far end from the dais, its outline still visible in the stonework of the wall. The aisles are supported on clustered shafts of handsome Purbeck marble.

At the east end, an imaginative Victorian magistrate commissioned a mural with the names of all Hampshire's MPs. The other end displays the celebrated 'King Arthur's Round Table'. The magnificence of this medieval furniture is sadly diminished by its name. It has nothing to do with a putative King Arthur; the wood has been dated to the turn of the 14th century. It was probably constructed in the hall and was first hung on the wall – why? who knows – in 1348. Its decoration is Tudor, as indicated by the white rose enclosed by the red. The portrait of King Arthur is said to bear a striking resemblance to the young Henry VIII. The table was last taken down for examination in 1976.

The lighting of the hall is worthy of *son et lumière*. The statue of Queen Victoria by Sir Alfred Gilbert portrays the queen regal on her throne but lit as if in a horror movie. At the east end are steel gates of an elegant modern design, installed in 1981 to celebrate the wedding of the Prince of Wales and Lady Diana Spencer.

Behind the hall is Queen Eleanor's charming garden, based on a 13th-century illuminated manuscript. It has Gothic arches, turf seats, a herb border and an arbour. Each of the flowers had romantic or religious significance – roses, lilies, columbines and strawberries. It is a pleasant diversion from the sound and fury within.

St Cross hospital

✯ ✯ England's oldest continuing almshouse, still home to a secular brotherhood

2 miles S of Winchester; private house, open all year

St Cross is one of England's oldest charitable institutions, set in the water meadows of the River Itchen outside Winchester. The hospital was founded in 1136 to support 'thirteen poor men, feeble and so reduced in strength that they can scarcely, or not at all, support themselves'. They should receive a bed, food and clothing and 'drink in sufficient quantity'. Most of the present domestic buildings date from Cardinal Beaufort in 1445.

A daily allowance was stipulated as a loaf of bread, three quarts of small beer, pottage of milk and bread, and a dish of flesh or fish according to the season. This surely must have supported more than just one person. In addition, 'one hundred other poor persons, as deserving as can be found and more indigent, shall be received at the hour of dinner'. Even they were entitled to three quarts of beer. Nor was this all. Money was allowed for a Master, steward, four chaplains, thirteen clerks, seven choristers and 'sundry servants'.

The relevant endowment to support this generosity became the cause of much mischief. St Cross became a byword for corruption, surviving the Dissolution under the patronage of the Bishops of

Left The 12th-century church of St Cross is all that remains of the original hospital buildings. This view is from the Master's garden.

Above There are lodgings at St Cross for 25 brothers, each one with his own self-contained flat. Those brothers wearing black robes are part of the charitable foundation of St Cross, set up in 1136 by Henry de Blois. The brothers dressed in red belong to the Order of Noble Poverty, established by Cardinal Henry Beaufort in 1445.

Winchester only since it was a lay foundation. The Master appeared able to pocket much of the revenue and not even attend at all. One absentee Master, the Earl of Guildford, relative of the then Bishop of Winchester, lifted an estimated £250,000 from the accounts in the early 19th century, leading to a Parliamentary outcry. St Cross was the most plausible model (of many) for Hiram's Hospital in Trollope's *The Warden*.

The place survived and today honours its founder's charter. The brothers still wear the traditional smock and cap. The wayfarer's dole is still dispensed to passing ramblers, 'a morsel of bread and a horn of beer'. The residential buildings are similar to those at Winchester College up the road, set round an outer more public courtyard and an inner residential one. A Tudor gatehouse leads into the outer quadrangle past the site of the Hundred Men's Hall. This was for the so-called out-pensioners. On the right is the old kitchen and ahead the 15th-century Beaufort Tower and porter's lodge, where the dole was and is dispensed.

The inner quadrangle is dominated by the Norman church of St Cross towering over its south-east corner. On the north side is the 14th-century Brethren's Hall, formerly the Great Hall of the Master's House. It still has its old screen and central hearth unaltered. Here the brothers ate and gathered, as they still do for occasional feasts. The minstrels' gallery survives, as do the steps to the Master's private rooms. Was a welfare state ever as lavish as this?

On the east side is an ambulatory beneath what was the old infirmary, prettily timbered with brick facings. Opposite, on the west side, are the present brothers' dwellings, built in the 15th century and a magnificent work of medieval domestic architecture. Each staircase has four sets of three rooms, each having a bold Tudor chimney. The brothers themselves act as eloquent guides.

The surroundings of St Cross are still blessedly tranquil. A Victorian visitor rightly remarked that this 'is where a good man, might he make his choice, would wish to die'.

Isle of

Osborne House

Wight

Isle of Wight

Appuldurcombe house

✶ Once the Isle of Wight's greatest house, built in William-and-Mary style, now a ruin

Near Wroxall, 6½ miles SE of Newport; English Heritage, open part year

Appuldurcombe is a ruin but you would not think so from a distance. The façade is of a great Baroque mansion set in a park designed by Capability Brown. Its rooms once looked out through stately cedars to the sloping hillside across the valley, as Brown intended.

Appuldurcombe (the stress is on the last syllable) was the ancestral home of the Worsleys, a branch of the family that now lives in Hovingham Hall (North Yorkshire). James Worsley was Keeper of the Wardrobe under Henry VIII and was awarded the military Captaincy of the Isle of Wight, marrying Anne Leigh, heiress of Appuldurcombe. His descendant, Sir Robert Worsley, returned from the Grand Tour in 1690, married a Thynne of Longleat, and decided to rebuild his family seat.

No sooner was the new house complete than Worsley fortunes swiftly declined. By the 19th century, the house was unoccupied except for visitors coming to see the pictures. In 1855, it was stripped and put on the market. It became successively a hotel, a school, a barracks and, after a bomb fell nearby in the Second World War, a ruin. This was stabilized in 1952 and restored to its present state in 1986. The main hall and a few downstairs rooms have been re-roofed and the façades and windows made to appear intact. That is all. It is the island's answer to The Grange (see page 84), but with no opera.

The architect of Appuldurcombe is unknown. It was a work of metropolitan sophistication in the style of Wren. Various experts have suggested John James, under the influence of Vanbrugh. As often with a William-and-Mary house, the side pavilions project forward and the central façade recedes. The entrance doorway has no pediment and is thus weaker than the pavilions. There is a colonnade to the south elevation.

Appuldurcombe was the finest and most original house on the island. Its shell has been beautifully and expansively restored. I cannot see what purpose is served by not restoring and tenanting the interior.

Brading: Rectory mansion

★ Tudor house with re-created interiors, set round a courtyard

At Brading, 7 miles E of Newport; museum, open all year

This place requires a deep breath. Buried within a brazen tourist attraction is what claims to be the only surviving Tudor building on the island. Tudor it certainly is. The Rectory Mansion and its adjacent inn sit round a picturesque courtyard, cluttered with a gallery, a well, seats, settles and Coke machines. The building must be enjoyed while we avert our eyes from a zoo of stuffed animals, Henry VIII and a corpse rising from its coffin. The Isle of Wight Waxworks Museum is way over the top and very popular.

The general horror has as its backdrop well-reinstated Tudor interiors, filled with beams, ancient partitions and tiny windows. In the pub section, an exhausted ostler is resting his feet in

water. The bedroom in which Louis de Rochefort was reputedly killed by a mysterious assassin looks much as it must have done in 1640.

The skivvy's attic bedroom re-creates the cramped conditions in which servants lived in such houses. The skivvy is naked apart from one stocking, for reasons best known to the museum's marketing director. In another bedroom, 'Little Jane' is dying, surrounded by her dog, a rose, prayer book and the curate for consolation. Apparently the scene is authentic to the house.

In the attic another real incident is depicted. A chimney-sweep's boy is stuck in the chimney with no means of escape. He eventually died here. It is as realistic as it is horrific.

Carisbrooke castle

At Carisbrooke, 1 mile SW of Newport; English Heritage, open all year

Few castles are more romantic than Carisbrooke. Its site dominates the centre of the island. 'He who holds Carisbrooke holds the Isle of Wight', went the saying. Given the strategic importance of the island in the Middle Ages, this was power. Elizabeth I gave the governorship to her cousin, Sir George Carey, to defend it against the Spanish.

The castle was again a centre of attention in 1647–8, when it imprisoned Charles I between the Civil War and his execution. This had been Charles's wish. Having escaped from Hampton Court he wished to remain on British soil and duly put himself under the care of the island's governor, much to the latter's embarrassment.

Left The outer gate bears the date 1900 and the initial 'B', for Princess Beatrice (1857–1944), Queen Victoria's youngest daughter, who restored the castle.

Charles was free to ride round the island. But various hamfisted attempts at helping him escape led to his being removed to London and his eventual execution.

The place then settled into gentle decay until Queen Victoria appointed her son-in-law, Prince Henry of Battenberg, as governor. After his death in 1896 from malaria, contracted in Africa, his wife, Princess Beatrice, took on the office herself and was to drastically restore the castle as her summer residence.

The building is impressive from a distance, its grey stone walls encircling the crest of a hill with land dropping steep on three sides. Entry over the moat is by a stone bridge through a battered gatehouse. Beyond lies an informal group of buildings of all periods. The interiors are disappointing, largely due to a clash between the Victorian museum installed by Princess Beatrice and English Heritage's house style.

The medieval hall still stands but was divided by the Elizabethan, George Carey, into

Above What was once the private chapel of medieval Carisbrooke now contains an 18th-century staircase leading to an upstairs room on the site of the former solar. A squint can still be found in the solar wall that would have offered medieval inhabitants of the castle a view of the chapel altar.

two floors. It retains a 14th-century fireplace next to a charming window seat. Carey almost obliterated an old chapel at the far end of the hall when he inserted a floor but fragments are discernible. An 18th-century staircase occupies the chapel space. All this has been heavily modernized.

Upstairs is the constable's lodging. Only some of the rooms are accessible, but these include Princess Beatrice's bedroom and the chamber where Charles I's daughter, Elizabeth, died of a chill. The rest of the upper storey is a museum devoted to the Isle of Wight generally and Carisbrooke specifically. Outside is the old well-house, its buckets raised by a donkey treadmill, although earlier by prisoners. The well is still in working order and donkeys perform regularly in the summer. The chapel is another of Princess Beatrice's works, a lovely chamber of early 20th-century Perpendicular. The walk round the castle walls is spectacular.

Morton manor

⭐ Age-old manor house filled with antiques and treasures

Near Brading, 7 miles E of Newport; private house, currently for sale

Janusz Trzebski, a Polish immigrant who served with the RAF, bought Morton Manor after the Second World War. He filled his house with whatever he could find from local houses that had fallen on hard times. His taste was wildly eclectic, from the exquisite to the kitsch. I am sure that one day everything will prove of value.

The house interior is so complex as to be hard to read. A medieval core leads to a Tudor longhouse, rebuilt in the late 17th century and altered since. The drawing room has a lovely Adam-style mantelpiece. In the dining room is Jacobean panelling supposedly removed from a galleon, some of its cracks still containing nautical caulking. The pretty library has original fabric wall-hangings. Everything is dominated by the clutter of objects which fill every shelf, bracket and tabletop. Morton is an antique shop waiting to happen. But it is also a family home, and the more jolly for its eccentricity.

The gardens are arranged round the house, with formal gardens below and rhododendrons and wilderness above. The Trzebski family established a vineyard at Morton and made award-winning wines. They also set up a wine-making museum in an old granary on the main lawn.

Left Set high on the wall above the fireplace in the dining room are the crests of the four families who have owned Morton Manor to date. To the left is the crest of the d'Aulas, a Norman family who arrived with William the Conqueror. Next to this is the Oglander crest, then that of the Fardells, who owned Morton from the mid-19th century until 1940. To the far right (half visible) is the crest of the Trzebski family. **Below** A Louis XV ormolu clock, after Sevres, is among the treasures that line the Robert-Adam-style fireplace in the drawing room.

Nunwell house

Nunwell sits comfortably surrounded by park on a hillside overlooking the Solent. On a fine day the grandstand at Goodwood can be seen on the South Downs. Here Oglanders were granted land by William the Conqueror in the 11th century. They served king and country, sheltered Charles I and commanded the island's militia. Their tombs fill Brading church. Sir John Oglander exhorted people in the 17th century to 'fear God, as we did; marry a wife one can'st love; keep out of debt; see the grounds well-stocked; and thou mayest live as happily at Nunwell as any Prince in the World'.

A descendant lives on the estate today, having occupied the main house until 1982 when he sold it to Colonel and Mrs Aylmer, who now open it to the public.

Nunwell is a fine example of a country gentleman's house, filled not with great works of art but with family pictures and furniture acquired over generations and with taste. Most are Oglander, some are Aylmer. The outside walls look as though they were made from a selection of English biscuits, in browns, creams and ochres. Georgian symmetry faces downhill, where the walls are of grey bricks and redbrick dressings. To the rear all is different, a rubicund 17th-century façade with bold doorway and big windows flanked by heavy wings. All we know is that the house was begun in 1607 and has been growing ever since.

Access is behind a Victorian extension, which means walking through the house from the latest period and ending with the earliest, a strange sensation. The music room is Edwardian and is filled with Oglander portraits. The dining room is Victorian, with an equestrian picture of an Aylmer driving his coach in Ireland. The drawing room and library, built or rebuilt in the 1760s, face out over the terrace. Paintings include Van Dyck's

'Nunwell is a **fine example** of a country **gentleman's** house ...'

Above Built in 1762, Nunwell's library features a finely decorated plaster ceiling, patterned with garlands of flowers and acanthus scrolls. The bookcases were created specifically for this room by the estate carpenter in 1765.
Right The hall is in the Jacobean part of Nunwell, built some time during the early 17th century. The ceiling here is papier mâché and dates to c1700.

'sunflower' self-portrait, showing the artist as an ardent Royalist. The library has Chippendale-style bookcases made by a local carpenter.

The entrance hall is the oldest part of the building, low, rich and Jacobean. It was reputedly here that Charles I dined on his last day of freedom before being taken to Carisbrooke, imprisonment and eventual death. Upstairs is the bedroom in which he slept with the equerry's tiny room next door. It is a poignant chamber. A small military museum recalls Colonel Aylmer's regiment, the Irish Guards, and the family's distinguished record as soldiers.

Nunwell's glory is its park and woodlands. Cedars and oaks dot the landscape towards the direction of the sea. They nod their heads gently in the wind while foolish tourists ignore them and stream along the coast. This is an Isle of Wight that I feel might be a distant colony.

Osborne house

★★★★ Victoria and Albert's summer retreat, restored as a memorial to the Queen and her family

Near East Cowes, 3½ miles N of Newport; English Heritage, open all year

There is no doubt where lies the emotional heart of this remarkable house. The Queen's massive canopied bed lies as it did on the day of her death. On Albert's side, his portrait lies on its pillow. Above it hangs the bag for his watch. After his death, the Queen never slept without them beside her. She died on the daybed here in 1901, with her vast family round her. The room was kept as a family shrine for half a century.

Osborne is the most eccentric of England's royal palaces. It was the home of only one monarch, Victoria, and is a memorial not just to her but to the Victorian family in general. We see her and her husband working together, playing together and enjoying their nine children. We also see where, for almost forty years, the Queen mourned her dead husband. Osborne is England's true Victoria and Albert Museum.

The house stands prominently in a park on a wooded bluff overlooking the Solent. It was designed in 1846 by Albert himself, six years into their marriage. Albert said the setting reminded him of the Bay of Naples. The Queen wrote in 1852 of the 'calm deep blue sea, the balmy air, all quite Italian'. After Albert's early death in 1861, it became Victoria's haven. She returned here for ever longer holidays, sometimes for three months each year. After her death, the house was never used again and still evokes the sadness of her old age. It is a place of memories, through which her multitudinous family might later have wandered, recalling happy childhood incidents.

Albert designed the exterior in association with the London builder of Belgravia, Thomas Cubitt. Although the main villa is symmetrical – indeed, it might be an Italianate house in Belgrave Square – later wings sprawled over the hillside to accommodate courtiers and staff. After the Queen's death, these wings became a convalescent home and naval college. Their future remains uncertain. The main house opened to the public in 1954.

The interiors have been restored as a virtuoso display of Victorian taste. They were mostly decorated by Albert, this time with his German art adviser, Ludwig Grüner. Ceilings and cornices, brightly coloured, are set above Italian and German sculpture and furniture. Osborne is never French and rarely English.

Entry is at the end of the Grand Corridor, a gallery of classical sculpture, its frieze a scaled-down copy of the Elgin Marbles. At its end are the Council Chamber and Audience Room for Privy Council meetings. In the corridor stands the Marine Venus in a shell niche. It came from the Baths of Caracalla in Rome and was bought by Albert at the great Stowe sale in 1848. Before entering the central Pavilion, visitors are treated to a fascinating diversion. They must dive downstairs to the Table Deckers' Room and Servery, as if looking beneath the bonnet of a car. Here is an underworld packed with tools of the server's trade: crockery, cutlery, sharpeners, cloths, sinks, china and glass galore. Is this wealth of equipment really never used any more?

The first of the Pavilion rooms is the dining room. The table is being laid by staff using measuring rods to get the precise settings. Their work is overlooked by copies of Winterhalter's great portraits of Victoria and her family, the embodiment of Victoriana. Yet the rooms are not overgrand. The one drawing room is designed with the billiard table in one arm, so that men are not completely segregated from ladies after dinner. Here family and guests gathered for music, games and conversation. Visitors often commented on the informality, a contrast with the normal image of Victoria's court. The rooms were designed by Albert in an extravagant Italianate style, the ceiling in a wild neo-Rococo.

The staircase is the one space in the Pavilion that merits the term palatial. Opposite the Page's Alcove, with its myriad bells, is a fresco by Dyce of Neptune resigning his dominion over the seas to Britannia. The landing gives onto Albert and Victoria's bedroom suite. This comprises their separate dressing rooms and bathrooms but joint bedroom and sitting room. Everything – toiletries, notepaper, even flushing lavatories – is still in

Left Queen Victoria learnt to play billiards on the table designed by Prince Albert for Osborne's drawing room. The legs and base were painted to look like marble, an example of superb craftsmanship and of Albert's economy with materials. **Below left** The mughal-style Durbar Room celebrates Victoria's title of Empress of India. Although she never visited India, the Queen took a keen interest in the country. **Below right** Affairs of state were never far away, even in a family retreat. The Queen and the Prince would often work side by side at their desks in her sitting room.

place. In the Queen's sitting room, with sweeping views over the Solent, are the adjacent desks at which she and Albert sat next to each other, working on state papers. He was always her 'private and personal secretary'.

On the second floor are the children's rooms, permitting easy access for their parents from below. The day and night nurseries have been restored from old photographs. They include a row of cribs and cots under the command of the Superintendent of the Royal Children, Lady Lyttelton. At the age of six, each would graduate from nursery to schoolroom. Downstairs is the Horn Room, furnished almost entirely from antlers, including a set of most uncomfortable chairs. Here hangs Landseer's painting of Victoria in black on a black horse, held by her much-loved servant, John Brown. Its title is *Sorrow*, though the ladies-in-waiting look unduly relaxed.

The final Durbar Room was added in 1890, in honour of the Queen's new status as Empress of India. It gave Osborne what it lacked, a formal state dining room. The decoration is astonishing, Indian mughal in style, designed by Bhai Ram Singh and John Lockwood Kipling, father of Rudyard. Although ivory in appearance, the walls and ceilings are of plaster and papier mâché, with doors and woodwork of teak. The room is now used for an exhibition of Indian gifts, received on Queen Victoria's Golden and Diamond Jubilees, and is sadly no longer used for banquets.

Albert's terraces at Osborne are paved with 'metallic lava', a 19th-century material intended to look like real lava. The copies of Italian statues are made of cement, Albert always being economical in his materials. The original parterres have been re-created, including such fiercely coloured Victorian favourites as hyacinths and pansies.

Osborne House:
The Swiss cottage

★★ Superior Wendy house built by Prince Albert for the Royal children

Near East Cowes, 3½ miles N of Newport; English Heritage, open all year

Albert was an obsessive father. He wanted his children to grow up as normal as possible, and in 1850 he gave them a corner of Osborne for their own. Here they would cook and keep house, 'entertain' their parents and meet their friends. In the garden they grew vegetables to sell to their father at the going market rate. This was to be a citadel of childhood independence.

The cottage was built in the then fashionable Swiss style. Investigation has shown the logs to be American and joined with metal ties. The kitchen still has the range and utensils used by the children. Upstairs is the dining room furnished, as is most of the cottage, in American birch with bobbin-turned legs. Against the wall is a writing desk at which Victoria is said to have continued working even when supposedly being entertained by her children.

The adjacent sitting room is less cosy: it was intended to be a small museum for which Albert encouraged the children to collect specimens and works of vernacular art. So many were collected – or donated – that most have been moved to a separate museum next door. The model shop front of Spratt the Grocer is still in place, with a selection of Victorian teas and wines.

We do not know how much the cottage was really enjoyed by the children, or how far it was more the fantasy of a well-meaning Teutonic father. It certainly shows Albert as a modern parent, eager to make Osborne a family home away from the pressure of Court. He described himself at Osborne as 'part forester, part builder, part farmer and part gardener'.

Below the cottage is Queen Victoria's bathing machine. This was once used as a chicken coop but is now restored to regal glory.

Yarmouth castle

☆ Last fortress in Henry VIII's chain of coastal defences

At Yarmouth, 9 miles W of Newport; English Heritage, open part year

'It all **feels** very **Tudor.**'

Yarmouth is the most personable of the coastal forts built by Henry VIII against attack from the Continent. It was completed in 1547, with a square rather than round bastion design. Its guns were trained over the Solent, flanking those of Hurst Castle (see page 92) opposite. Now the best thing they can do is survey the yachts in the harbour below.

The castle today has the familiar Henrician gun platform, with a field of fire to left and right. The entrance was from the foreshore but is now down an inviting alley from the centre of the little town. This passes over the site of the moat and directly into the living quarters. These are in a tight courtyard, made smaller by the extension of the higher gun platform in the early 17th century. It all feels very Tudor.

The interior has a domesticity rare in the Henrician forts. To the left is the cellar where the gunners lived. To the right is the Master Gunner's house, with hall and parlour, well supplied with fireplaces. The kitchen is in the bastion beyond, with a bedroom upstairs. This is a proper house. A second storey, mostly a single long room, was added in the 17th century. The rooms are sadly bare.

Wilt

Longleat

shire

Wiltshire

Avebury manor

At Avebury, 6 miles W of Marlborough; National Trust, open part year

I prefer Avebury to Stonehenge. Its stone circles and avenues are scattered round the old village, looming beside the road and behind back gardens. They are like Don Giovanni's Commendatore, the past eager to grasp us in a clammy hand. The early Christians founded a monastery outside the circle to avoid (or appease) its pagan demons. This may have formed the basis of the present manor.

Avebury was bought in 1547 by William Sharington of neighbouring Lacock Abbey (see page 146), possibly on the profits of clipping the coinage at the Bristol Mint, a crime for which he just escaped execution. The manor was later a farmhouse, until being restored in 1902 by Leopold and Nora Jenner. They made Avebury a model of vernacular restoration. Hudson remarked on its 'true note of homeliness ... with enough variety of style and character to give a sense of continuous habitation'.

After 1935, the house frequently changed hands. It was left empty for years although various commercial uses were planned. It was acquired by the National Trust in 1991 and refurnished by tenants, but lacks the character of its more celebrated contemporaries. A lecture tour of just the five rooms on view is compulsory, where none is needed.

The entrance leads into a screens passage with a library to the left and hall to the right. The latter, lit by large Elizabethan windows, was modernized in the early 18th century with classical doors and panelling. It is rather bleak. The two best rooms are upstairs, the Tudor Bedroom and the Great Chamber above the hall. The overmantel in the former is c1600, its scrollwork and arcaded panel complementing a curvilinear ceiling. In the Great Chamber the embroidery of the bed covers was by Mrs Jenner, whose ubiquitous needlework is outstanding.

The best feature of Avebury is its garden, with a circular yew border. This was laid out by the Jenners in the style of Gertrude Jekyll, strongly architectural and well maintained.

Bowood house

★★ Fragmentary remains of a Robert Adam house

Near Calne, 4 miles SE of Chippenham; private house, open part year

When the 8th Marquess of Lansdowne retired from Bowood to Perthshire in 1972, he warned his son that 'you may find maintaining the house and estate quite a challenge'. It was a challenge he had considerably eased in 1955 by flattening Henry Keene and Robert Adam's so-called Big House and retreating into the Little House, an extension at the back.

Lansdowne had inherited Bowood from a cousin who had died in the Second World War, but even in the 1950s the demolition was controversial. The family's Lansdowne House in Berkeley Square had been demolished before the war. To demolish two great houses inside a generation was going too far. Adam's Bowood dining room is now bizarrely suspended halfway up Lloyd's of London in Leadenhall Street.

Above The Terrace Gardens at Bowood were commissioned by the 3rd Marquess. The upper terrace, designed by Sir Robert Smirke, was finished in 1818 and the lower, by George Kennedy, was added in 1851. Overlooking the lower terrace steps is a sculpture of a recumbent female nude by David Wynne, commissioned by the Lord Lansdowne in 1978.

Above An Adam-style door, originally from the drawing room of the Big House at Bowood, opens onto a Sculpture Gallery. The gallery was created in 1980 from a row of stables, but during the time of the 1st Marquess (1737–1805) this area housed a menagerie – an orang-utan and a leopard were among the wild animals on show. Today, the room displays part of the 18th-century Lansdowne collection of classical marbles, as well as tapestries and pieces by 19th-century sculptors.

The Marquess's son, the Earl of Shelburne, converted the fragmentary remains of the property into a country estate run as a business concern. He lives in the Little House and has redecorated Adam's Diocletian Orangery and screen as an art gallery and museum. The screen was designed to conceal the service courtyards, and now supplies an architectural backdrop to the formal gardens.

The Orangery is open to the public. Its gallery is filled with Old Masters and historical and contemporary works. In the middle is a chapel, erected in the 19th century by C. R. Cockerell. The reredos frames a central Madonna, adapted from an organ case reputedly by William Kent.

At one end of the Orangery is Cockerell's neo-classic library, converted from a surviving Adam room. It is a virtuoso chamber, warmly decorated with ceiling medallions of classical writers and fine Wedgwood urns on the bookcases. The Orangery's other end leads through Adam-style doors, rescued from the Big House, into a Sculpture Gallery that was once part of the stables.

A series of exhibition rooms follow. These include a reproduction Georgian room with effigies, costumes and original pictures and furniture. Upstairs is the Bowood collection of watercolours, with works by Turner, Varley, Lear and Bonington, and a room of Napoleonic treasures, including the Emperor's death mask.

Corsham court

✦✦ Tudor mansion with a magnificent collection of Old Masters

At Corsham, 4 miles SW of Chippenham; private house, open part year

Corsham Court lies in one of the prettiest towns in Wiltshire, glimpsed from afar across a vista of parkland. Owned by one family, the Methuens, since the 18th century, it is guarded by a skirting of parish church, voluptuous yews and 16th-century riding school. Its Elizabethan walls have received the attention of Robert Smythson (possibly), Capability Brown, Humphry Repton, John Nash and Thomas Bellamy, yet the original character of the house has somehow survived. It is filled with a prodigious collection of Old Masters.

The house was begun by an Elizabethan merchant, Thomas Smythe, in 1582 with sufficient echoes of Longleat to suggest the hand of Robert Smythson. In 1745, the property was bought by

Above The Picture Gallery is among the Corsham rooms designed in the 1760s by Capability Brown. Proportionally, the room is a triple cube, some 72ft long. At one end is a studio copy of Van Dyck's *Charles I on Horseback*; the adjacent wall displays his *Betrayal of Christ*. Over the mantel is a work from the Rubens studio, *A Wolf and Fox Hunt*.

Paul Methuen, descendant of a Bradford-on-Avon clothier. He had Capability Brown extend the building to display his collection of Italian and Dutch paintings. In the 1840s, these were augmented by the Sanford bequest of Old Masters after the marriage of Frederick Methuen to Horatia Sanford in 1844. This required a Victorian north front by Bellamy, a copy of the Elizabethan south front.

The interiors are a little cold, as if the main rooms had been turned over to a museum and the family fled (which is not true). Visiting Corsham is like visiting an elderly great-aunt, albeit a magnificent one.

The state rooms are now filled with the paintings and furniture of a Georgian man of taste. The picture gallery contains van Dyck's *Betrayal of Christ* and in the Cabinet Room is a Filippo Lippi *Annunciation*. The Octagon Room, albeit no longer so shaped, contains a beautiful sculpture of a sleeping Cupid and there are two superb Rococo mirrors in the Bedroom. There are also works by Claude, del Sarto and Guercino. The corridors and halls are lined with display cases of porcelain.

Corsham has fine grounds and an arboretum. Apart from the yews to the west and a lake to the east, the drooping arms of an oriental plane on the lawn are 240ft in perimeter. Beyond is the Cold Bath House built by Capability Brown in 1761, a charming Gothick conceit and a handsome landscape.

Froxfield: **Somerset** hospital

✦ Almshouse set round a quadrangle with Gothick chapel at the centre

At Froxfield, 6 miles E of Marlborough; private house, viewing by arrangement

This is one of the largest and grandest of 17th-century almshouses. The founder was the Duchess of Somerset in 1694. The ranges are set round a long rectangular garden with a smart Regency Gothick chapel in the middle, far more generous than the customary pokey quadrangle. The hospital sits on the A4, the former Great West Road, and is as enticing a place to end one's days as I can imagine.

The building is clearly of two periods. The early ranges are to the right of the entrance gate with stone-mullioned windows. The range to the left has identical roofs and dormers but the windows are no longer stone but wood. This later work is dated 1775, by when the original design must have seemed exceptionally old-fashioned.

The chapel, dated 1813, in the courtyard is delightful. It has bold pinnacles and a whimsical panel of crocketed gables on the side facing the entrance.

The hospital was intended to serve the needs of twenty retired clergy and thirty lay widows. It still does.

'... as enticing a place to end one's days as I can imagine.'

Great Chalfield manor

★★★ Medieval manor, complete with moat, gatehouse and church

Near Broughton Gifford, 4 miles N of Trowbridge; National Trust, open part year

Great Chalfield has long been a front runner in the 'best medieval manor' stakes. It sits in a Wiltshire countryside as yet unpolluted by development. There is a moat, gatehouse and barn to guard its beauty and an adjacent church to guard its soul. Such houses have at some time needed a kindly restorer. Great Chalfield's was Robert Fuller, a local businessman who bought it in 1878 and began restoration in 1905.

The house was built *c*1470 on the profit of wool, that of Thomas Tropnell, clothier and lawyer. The layout was traditional, a hall house with a courtyard to the rear. What was novel was that the services and kitchens were pushed to the back. The front thus has not one but two 'family' wings either end of the Hall, both gabled and with elegant Perpendicular oriels. One gable is crowned with an armed soldier, the other with a dog and monkey.

By the 19th century, the solar wing was derelict and the Great Hall was divided into farm workers' quarters. Fuller set about rescuing the place. He had the local architect, Harold Brakspear, completely rebuild the solar wing, which gives visitors the familiar West Country problem of disentangling Edwardian work from medieval. The house passed to the National Trust as an early gift in 1943, but with the Fuller family, now the Floyds, in continued residence. On my last visit, the rooms were very much occupied, the Great Hall recovering from a teenage party.

This Great Hall still rises the full height of the building. Its interior is of the original proportions, but has been Edwardianized, with a new minstrels' gallery above a reproduction screen. High on some of the walls are grimacing viewing masks, peepholes through which ladies might have watched what was happening below.

To the right of the entrance is Tropnell's dining room, with an Elizabethan plaster ceiling and panelling. On the wall is a mural painting, believed to be of Tropnell himself. The figure is shown with five fingers plus a thumb, considered to be a sign of covetousness. If it is indeed Tropnell, this is the earliest picture of a Member of Parliament in England. Above the dining room is a bedroom with an ante-room over the porch; this contains a concealed bath

Below The archways at the eastern end of the Great Hall lead into two bays, each with a room above. These upper rooms each have a viewing mask overlooking the Hall below. The mask on the north side is of a king with ass's ears; to the south, is a bishop. At the western end of the Hall is the minstrels' gallery, overlooked by a third mask of a laughing face.

Above Great Chalfield's east wing was demolished in 1838, but its north wall and the East Oriel window that lit the solar were left standing. Careful drawings of the manor house had been made in 1836, which proved of great help to the architect, Harold Brakspear, when reconstruction of the wing began in 1905.

tub. In the bedroom window are depicted two birds advising, 'Love God, drede shame, desire worship and kepe thy name.' Name was a synonym for everything from reputation to boy heirs.

At the other end of the Great Hall is the solar, as rebuilt in the 1900s. The upper chamber is a re-creation of the original, Brakspear being meticulous in his archaeology. The semi-circular oriel window is a conceit of fan vaults and pendants. It offers a view over the front courtyard and little church belfry, a placid English scene.

South of the house, beyond the footings of the old quadrangle, the land falls away towards former stew ponds. The roses are undiluted by hybrids, as English as the house itself.

Hamptworth lodge

★ ★ Edwardian house in Jacobean-revival style, with woodwork by an owner-enthusiast

At Hamptworth, 10 miles SE of Salisbury; private house, open part year for tours only

In 1910, the wealthy Edwardian eccentric, Harold Moffatt, bought Hamptworth Lodge, took one look at it and cried, 'Thank God, dry rot!' He demolished the place and, with the architect Guy Dawber, built a new Jacobethan mansion. It had all modern conveniences and a spacious internal layout.

Moffatt made almost all the interior carpentry and furniture himself. Although he also rebuilt Goodrich Court in Herefordshire, Hamptworth was his masterpiece. As the classicists had striven to re-create Palladio at Chiswick House (London), so Moffatt strove to re-create the Middle Ages. Hamptworth must be England's most remarkable display of amateur cabinet-making, if amateur is the word.

The exterior displays a fanatical revivalism. The walls are timber-framed. Some windows have stone mullions, some wood. Gables sweep down on all sides, with large chimneys rising above them. Entry is into a screens passage with a staircase hall and gallery. This forms the heart of the house. Two downstairs drawing rooms, one for men, one for women, are entirely neo-Tudor. The furniture is either 'period' or Moffatt reproduction.

The dining room table and sideboard are by Moffatt, as are the oak chairs with strapwork. So too are the dressers, one of them inlaid with mother-of-pearl. Some of the bedroom ceilings are barrel-vaulted, others have complex Jacobean plasterwork. The largest room in the house is the Great Hall with an unusual roof construction. It houses a Willis organ and has a wooden screen, again by Moffatt.

Many rooms display 'apprentice pieces', miniatures made by young carpenters as advertisements. They were favourites in Moffatt's collection. The house is now owned by Moffatt's descendants, the Andersons, who are admirably respectful of his work.

Holt: The Courts

★ Georgian house now the focal point of an extensive garden

3 miles N of Trowbridge; National Trust garden, open part year

The Courts is a gem of a house. Its National Trust tenant from 1943 to 1990 was Moyra Goff, spinster daughter of the former owner. She adored the garden, planted its arboretum and raced her magnificent AC Cobra sports car up and down the street outside until she was well over eighty. Locals swore that she deliberately increased the speed commensurate with her age.

The house is small and the garden disproportionately large. Only the garden is at present open to the public, but the house façade is so integral to it as to make them seem one and the same creation. A small gateway leads from the main street into a short avenue of pleached limes. This is closed at the far end by the house's classical façade in warm Bath stone.

The Courts was built by a Quaker clothier in c1720 on the site of the old village court. He used the stream that flows through the garden to power a small mill, and to dye the finished cloth. The mill stream ran where the main lawn is now. He built onto his house a Georgian façade fit for a

Above The yew walk at The Courts runs between the terrace and the main lawn. Topiary is a recurring theme in the gardens and here large yews, simply clipped into bulbous conical shapes, line one side of the walk. Soft mounds of silvery grey cotton lavender fill the spaces in between and spill out over the path. In early autumn, red-hot pokers and *Verbena bonariensis* provide bright spots of colour.

gentleman. This is a delight, appearing rather as a façade with a house attached to the back.

The style is anything but Quaker. It might rather be termed Clothier's Baroque, with similar flourishes to those found on the chest tombs round the parish church of Painswick in Gloucestershire. The doorway has Tuscan columns and a curved broken pediment. The window pediment above has scrolls, flanked by more windows with broken pediments. It is all topped off with a bold gable. Pevsner called it all the product of 'a vulgar mind', art historian's snobbery.

The garden layout was started by Sir George Hastings after 1900, but within nine years he had sold the property to two ladies, Miss Barclay and Miss Trim, and then to Major Goff and his wife, Lady Cecilie. It was they who perfected the garden we see today, Lady Cecilie mapping the enclosed flower gardens. Her philosophy was that a garden should be a thing of mystery and not be seen entirely from one viewpoint. The Terrace has a topiary of dancing bears.

Lacock abbey

✦✦✦✧ Medieval nunnery preserved within Tudor and Gothick conversions

At Lacock, 3 miles S of Chippenham; National Trust, open part year

One gloomy winter afternoon during the Second World War, James Lees-Milne arrived at Lacock Abbey to negotiate its transfer to the National Trust. He found himself trapped. The spinster owner, Matilda Talbot, was maintaining her tradition of a regular *thé dansant* in the Great Hall. 'Where she collected her young ladies from, it is hard to say,' Lees-Milne recalled. 'All were exceedingly plain and utterly speechless. To an ancient gramophone which required winding every two minutes, we danced the Roger de Coverley while the fog swirled against the Gothick windows ...'

The music was a lament for the decline of the English house. Not since the 1539 Dissolution of the old nunnery had Lacock's fate seemed so hopeless as in the 1940s. Yet Lacock is with us still, complete with its estate and picture village. Talbots are in part occupation. This lovely house is secure once more.

With the closure of the monastery, Lacock passed to William Sharington, a rogue best known for debasing the coinage in the Bristol Mint and narrowly escaping execution. But he respected medieval architecture and was eager to convert rather than demolish his acquisition. Unlike most Tudor occupiers of monastic remains, he kept the conventual buildings in place, retaining the intimate, claustral atmosphere. Sharington's tower at Lacock of *c*1550 is a superb example of Tudor Renaissance, as is his tomb in the parish church.

Sharington was succeeded by his brother, whose daughter, Olive, fell in love with a Talbot from Shrewsbury, a descendant of the abbey's original founder. Defying her father's opposition, she is said to have leaped from the abbey roof into her lover's arms, saved from injury by her voluminous petticoats acting as a parachute. To this Lacock invention, a later Talbot, the Victorian William Henry Fox, added that of calotype photography. Grainy relics of his work can be seen throughout the house.

Above A view of Lacock Abbey, from the southeast over the Avon, taken by Fox Talbot in 1844. It appeared in his book *The Pencil of Nature*, the first book to be illustrated with photographs. **Left** The west front of the abbey as it looks today.

William Henry Fox Talbot
1800-77

Fox Talbot was something of a polymath, with interests in botany, etymology, mathematics and egyptology, but it was for his pioneering work in photography that he is most celebrated. Talbot took his first picture at Lacock in 1835 (see page 150) using a camera obscura and light-sensitive paper. Over the next few years he experimented with techniques until he developed a process that would allow the production of any number of prints from one original negative. More often than not, his subjects were Lacock Abbey and the surrounding area. Although he became well known as Fox Talbot, it was not the name he preferred to use and generally signed himself 'Henry Talbot'.

In 1753, John Ivory Talbot decided to gothicize the house, with the help of Sanderson Miller. It was one of the earliest instances of Georgian Gothick, and executed with panache. The Great Hall was converted into a chamber three bays wide, with a flowing double flight of steps to the front door. Cupolas and a decorative parapet adorn the façade. The interior of the hall is a Sanderson masterpiece, as if Robert Adam had been asked to decorate a French museum of the Middle Ages. Talbot had the arms of his friends emblazoned in the ceiling, to share in the glory of his creation. On the north wall is a

scapegoat, with a lump of sugar kept on its nose for almost a century, said to bring luck.

Lacock from this point on should be seen as two houses, one on the ground floor and formed of the former nunnery cloister, the other Tudor above. The upper residential floor contains the Sharington rooms, including the Brown Gallery, Stone Gallery, domestic apartments and South Gallery. The lower floor comprises the convent rooms, which Sharington left in place. They are a rare survival of a complete monastic set. These two layers are two unrelated houses, yet both pay obeisance to the building's history.

Below The Ante Room, or East Bedroom, is part of the suite of domestic rooms added by William Sharington. It is now decorated with mid-19th-century hand-printed wallpaper and furnished with a French Empire-style bed, complete with an ornate red canopy, trimmed with gold tassels. The door opens onto the short lobby, next to the Stone Gallery entrance.

The galleries are filled with Talbot impedimenta, some valuable, most merely quaint. In the Brown Gallery are medieval carvings from the old abbey and a portrait of Matilda Talbot, the last owner. The Stone Gallery was fashioned by Sharington from the old convent dormitory. It is like a medievalist's attic, a jumble of ancient stained glass, moose horns, funeral helms, a rocking horse and a fine set of Flemish shell-backed chairs. Portraits of the Gothick Talbot and his wife are by Dahl.

A group of 18th-century rooms forms the junction of the Stone Gallery and South Gallery.

In one is displayed a copy of the Magna Carta. The Lacock original, the only copy still legible, was presented by the Talbots to the British Museum in 1946. Such copies were sent to every county by Henry III and this alone survived. Sharington's octagonal tower contains his Strong Room with, in its centre, the carved stone Lacock Table, an outstanding work of 16th-century English Renaissance. It rests on a classical capital surrounded by four satyrs on pedestals. Its carver was reputedly John Chapman.

The long South Gallery was much altered by Fox Talbot in the 19th century. It contains portraits

Below The walls of the Great Hall are punctuated with Gothick niches hosting terracotta figures by the Austrian artist Victor Sederbach. Among the figures is the Scapegoat (**below right**), the creature that symbolically bore the sins of the Children of Israel and was sent out into the wilderness on the Day of Atonement (Leviticus 16: 21–22).

Above The nunnery at Lacock was founded in 1232 by Ela, Countess of Salisbury, as a home for Augustinian canonesses. The medieval North Cloisters are a clear indication of the prosperity of the Abbey before the Dissolution. **Below** Fox Talbot's first photograph, taken in 1835, of the oriel window in the South Gallery; the original was a negative image.

of Sharington and other family members. Here too is the window that appeared in Fox Talbot's first-ever photograph in 1835, a dim outline of light, wonderfully atmospheric.

The delight of Lacock is to wander from these busy, cluttered rooms downstairs to the serenely ascetic nunnery chambers. It is easy to see what fascinated owners, from the Elizabethans to the Victorians, with the medieval style. Here are fine vaulted rooms, with traceried windows and wall-paintings. Thanks to Sharington we have a memorial to what might have survived all over England, had it not been for the Dissolution.

The south cloister walk is worthy of a cathedral, with superb vault bosses. In the days of the nunnery, these were mostly service rooms for the living quarters above. They include the chaplain's room, sacristy, chapter house, warming room and rere-dorter. North of the main block is Sharington's stable courtyard, a charmingly unaltered work of the 16th century.

Little Clarendon

Little Clarendon needs a lit fire, a boiling kettle, a cat and an old lady. The house was a cottage and farmhouse from the 15th century, but was bought and restored in 1901 by the Reverend George Engleheart. His daughter, Catherine, recalled it as being in a 'dreadful state ... divided up between two families in a warren of passages and rooms like biscuit tins ... ceilings set to hide the old beams, and half the mullioned windows were built up'.

Within a year, Engleheart had returned the house to its medieval form and planted a charming cottage garden round it. He was an ardent breeder of daffodils, an obsession which 'drew him further away from clerical life'. His daffodils won him a medal from the Royal Horticultural Society, and still fill the garden in spring.

The house is in its 17th-century form. The two-storey porch gives onto what would have been the hall, with a medieval fireplace and low beams. To one side is the drawing room with vernacular furniture and more beams. The parlour or solar wing to the right is of three storeys with mullioned windows. The interior is furnished as the Englehearts left it, but the National Trust has scrubbed it within an inch of its life. All it needs is some rough edges.

Littlecote

★★★ A medieval and Elizabethan mansion with Roman remains in the grounds

Near Chilton Foliat, 8 miles E of Marlborough; now a hotel

The great medieval house of Littlecote belonged to the Darrell family until it fell into the hands of 'Wild Darrell'. A bullying, lawless local grandee, he found himself accused of infanticide, and gave the house as a bribe to a lawyer cousin, Sir John Popham, later Lord Chief Justice. Darrell died falling from a horse in 1589. It was Popham who built the main late-Elizabethan façade of c1600, but he left the earlier Darrell house to the rear as an architectural Siamese twin. This gives Littlecote an extraordinary back-to-front appearance.

Pophams held the house into the 20th century when it passed to the Wills family. Then in 1985 and amid much controversy, it passed to the tycoon, Peter de Savary, who briefly turned it into a Cromwellian theme park. This did not last but the Littlecote collection of 17th-century weapons was sold to the Royal Armories Museum. The house went to Warner Hotels, who are now trying to retrieve some of the armour.

Warners have saved many houses and gardens from a worse fate. Life has been breathed into once deserted interiors, which are more accessible than conversions into apartments. But 'mid-market hotel', as their literature claims, means what it says. Furniture and fittings tend to be institutional and all sense of original family occupation is lost. Littlecote needs to recapture its soul.

The front and rear are completely distinct. Popham's front is redbrick and E-plan, symmetrical and with tall windows on either side of the entrance. It is unadorned and dull, like a Victorian reproduction. The rear (shown below) is fascinating. It is not one façade but two lying side by side – owners of Littlecote could not bear to demolish anything. On the right is the earliest, medieval, house of the Darrells, an old-fashioned hall with gabled cross-wings. On the left of this, added by the father of 'Wild Darrell' in the 1530s, is an E-plan extension primarily housing an early Long Gallery. Much restored by later generations of Pophams, it has a hexagonal bay window as frontispiece and walls of flint.

The interior is similarly divided between the Popham rooms at the front and a warren of

Above Excavations at Littlecote in the 18th-century uncovered the remains of a Roman villa complex. Just south of the villa itself is a separate room that features this particularly fine mosaic floor, known as the Orpheus mosaic after the representation of Orpheus with his lyre in the central roundel. The room is believed to have been associated with the cult of Bacchus. The style of the figurative elements, the patterns of the mosaic, and the evidence of the surrounding structures, all suggest a date of around AD 360 for the floor.

medieval chambers behind. Popham's Great Hall has a fine Jacobean screen and plaster ceiling with pendants. The windows contain Continental stained glass and a love-knot of Henry VIII and Jane Seymour, who reputedly courted in this house (as in many others). The staircase was erected in the 19th century, when the kitchens were moved to a side wing. The drawing rooms are large and plain, although one has chinoiserie panels.

The rooms of the older house behind are exceptional. The Tudor chambers surviving from the Darrell house have been well conserved. They are entered from the library and begin with the Dutch Parlour. This enchanting room is entirely covered in panels painted by imprisoned Dutch seamen in the 1660s. They include scenes from *Don Quixote* and other Spanish legends and form a composition unlike any room in England.

A series of allegedly haunted rooms leads to a chapel, converted from the medieval hall. This survives as an unaltered Puritan preaching box, furnished in oak with pews, galleries and a pulpit where the altar would have been. The thin-seated pews were said to be designed so that any sleeper would 'drop off' them, hence the phrase. An oak staircase leads to Darrell's Long Gallery. This is again of oak, panelled and with thin pilasters. It carries a magnificent plaster frieze and a selection of Popham portraits.

Such was the Tudor revivalism of the Pophams that Littlecote never succumbed to naturalistic landscaping in the Capability Brown era. Despite the depredations of the 20th century, both de Savary and the present owners have beautifully restored the herbaceous borders and walled gardens. We await the return of the old house.

Longleat

English-Renaissance palace with interiors reworked in the 19th century

4 miles W of Warminster; private house, open all year

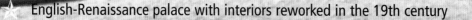

There is no finer sight in England than Longleat from the heights of Cranborne Chase on a late-autumn afternoon. The sun slants across the countryside. Animals, tame and wild, roam the park. The old house stands with the light full on its face, illuminating its walls with a golden flame. Architecture and nature are in total harmony.

Longleat was one of the great prodigy houses of the Elizabethan era, ranking with Wollaton Hall, near Nottingham, and Hardwick Hall in Derbyshire. The property was acquired by Sir John Thynne, later Steward to the Protector Somerset, in 1541. As befitted a servant of Edward VI, he was a

'There is **no finer** sight in **England** than Longleat...'

zealous Protestant whom the Catholic Mary I ordered to 'remain in his own country' during her reign. After a fire in 1567, Thynne, by now an Elizabethan courtier, decided to rebuild Longleat. It was known as 'the first well-built house in England', its design evolving swiftly during its construction from gabled Tudor mansion to the epitome of an English Renaissance palace.

Longleat drew inspiration from the pre-eminent building of the age, old Somerset House in London, for which Thynne had been responsible to his patron, Somerset. Of this period only the exterior, the Great Hall and a number of chimneypieces survive. The interior was completely remodelled by Sir Jeffry Wyatville in 1806–13 and redecorated by J. G. Crace in the 1870s.

Yet, while Crace's interiors at Longleat are effusively Victorian, they match as well as any revivalist house of the period the ostentation of the 16th-century exterior. Thynnes occupy the house to this day, with increasing eccentricity. In 1949, it was the first house to open commercially to the public, introducing 'the lions of Longleat' in 1966. The exotic paintings and other manifestations of the bohemian lifestyle of the present Marquess of Bath add greatly to its appeal.

Seen close to, the outside of Longleat is a severe façade of classical pilasters rising three storeys to the flat roof. The latter is astonishing, a crowded forest of domes, banqueting pavilions, ornamented chimneys, finials and scrollwork. Thynne's guests were expected to climb up after dinner and promenade and play games among these devices, high above the woods spread out below them. It might all be a stage-set for *A Midsummer Night's Dream*.

Given the ruthlessness with which the 19th century treated Longleat, the survival untouched of the Great Hall illustrates the sanctity that attached to these shrines of ancestral history. The Hall is still set off-centre, reached by a screens passage. The ceiling bears the arms of Thynnes down the centuries and is supported by

ten giant hammerbeams. The chimneypiece is original as are the panelling and minstrels' gallery. Even the original oak table remains, overlooked by the antlers of an Irish elk, now an extinct species whose remains were much beloved of Great Hall decorators everywhere.

From here on, the house is mostly of the 19th century. Modernization was carried out by the 2nd Marquess in the 1800s and his grandson in the 1870s. The first sought corridors and a grand staircase, to bring warmth and privacy to the rooms and ease of access for servants. The second wished to bring to his house the colour and romanticism of Italy. Seven of the main reception rooms are by Crace and are his masterpiece. Their only equal for Victorian Italianate is the grand suite at Alnwick Castle, in Northumberland.

The reception rooms on the ground floor are mostly libraries, seven in all. The house claims 40,000 books, the finest collection in Europe in private hands. The Red Library is Crace at his most vivid, with deeply embossed wall-coverings and gilded ceiling. No less extravagant is the breakfast room, with a superb Lawrence of the 1st Marquess and a Watts of the 4th Marchioness. Crace's ceiling to the dining room is more astonishing still, based on one in the Ducal Palace in Venice. Everywhere are Thynne portraits of all periods, including modern ones, often startlingly juxtaposed.

The rear corridors and stairs are decorated by the present Marquess. They include stained glass from the old chapel, modern paintings of his 'Wessex School' and an exhibition of the ravages of the voracious deathwatch beetle at Longleat. On the first floor are Crace's three great state rooms. His ceiling in the state dining room frames paintings by the school of Titian. A van Dyck depicts Isabella Rich, wife of Sir James Thynne in the reign of Charles I, who danced naked across old London Bridge. The room contains two exquisite Flemish ebony cabinets.

The saloon is formed from the old gallery, its ceiling based on the Palazzo Massimo in Rome and its fireplace based on one in the Doge's Palace. Flemish tapestries clothe the walls and Boulle furniture the floors. The drawing room ceiling takes us to the library of St Mark's Cathedral in Venice. Everything in this room is by Crace, apart from the Old Masters and furniture. His virtuosity as a 'revivalist' is as

Above and below Longleat's Safari Park opened in 1966 on the site of the Grove, a forest garden in the grounds where the 18th-century 2nd Viscount Weymouth had kept bears, wolves and a leopard. Lions were the first inhabitants of the modern park, but they were joined within a few months by zebras and giraffes. The Safari Boats were launched in 1967 to take visitors out onto the Half Mile Pond for a closer look at the Californian sea lions that live there.

accomplished as that of William Kent for the Palladians. Yet who knows anything of Crace?

Longleat now rambles on with a life of its own. A corridor is decked with family dresses and cabinets of Sèvres and Dresden. The Chinese Bedroom has handpainted wallpaper. In the old music room can be found a Terborch portrait; in the Prince of Wales's Bedroom two superb Ruisdaels. The circuit is completed by Wyatville's Grand Staircase, a theatrical promenade hung with flamboyant Snyders pictures and some of the finest hunting works of the under-appreciated John Wootton.

The best-known paintings at Longleat are the murals by the present 7th Marquess. These were begun in 1964, ten years after the aristocratic hippy took up residence in the west wing. They are now said to cover a third of the house interiors. They are presented as 'keyhole glimpses into my psyche', and include pictures of the Marquess's various 'wifelets' and the 'Kama Sutra Mural'. Mosaics on psychedelic themes are being prepared by the Marquess's nephew, Alexander Thynne. Some of this comes with a taste warning, but in years to come the murals will doubtless be seen as important works of late 20th-century art.

Longleat once lay at the centre of an extensive web of formal parterres. These were swept away in the 18th century by Capability Brown and Repton, but have in part been restored. A huge maze, reputedly the largest anywhere, has been built and others are promised. The astonishing Safari Park, which rescued Longleat's finances in the 1960s, is well screened from view. The Elizabethans would have found nothing strange in elephants, giraffes, lions and monkeys gliding and prancing past their façades. Longleat was always the architecture of the exotic.

Lydiard house

★★★ A Palladian-style mansion with Georgian decoration

At Lydiard Tregoze, 4 miles W of Swindon; museum, open all year

In 1873, the 5th Viscount Bolingbroke (and 6th Viscount St John) demanded that the loud hooter on the Great Western Railway's Swindon factory be silenced. Used to summon workers from nearby villages, the hooter woke him at 5.15 every morning. Since the workers lost pay if they were a minute late, the hooter was a local necessity and a petition of 4,339 names was raised to keep it. It was silenced on his lordship's request, with the help of a doctor witness. The nation rose in ridicule and the railway installed another hooter with a different note. His lordship was humiliated. It blew its last in 1986.

Right The 17th-century Huguenot painted window is the work of Abraham van Linge. Each diamond-shaped quarry features an individual image, painted on both sides of the glass to increase the three-dimensional effect. The window was probably moved to the boudoir from elsewhere in the house when Lydiard was remodelled in the 1740s.

This was not the first reverse suffered by the St John family. They inherited Lydiard House from the Beauchamps, whose old hall can still be seen in traces to the rear of the present house. Active in the Civil War, a St John saw three of his sons die for the King while two triumphed with Cromwell. A later St John rose to political prominence, and in 1712 was ennobled under the old family title of Bolingbroke.

Money was always short and the house which Bolingbroke rebuilt in 1743 was always in debt. By the 20th century, the family had retreated before advancing decay. When Lydiard was requisitioned in 1940, it was declared unfit even for military habitation. The family sold it to Swindon Corporation for £4,500. The interior was restored and it is now an excellent museum.

Lydiard was possibly designed by Roger Morris in the 1740s, the main façade in the style of Inigo Jones. A Palladian box is elaborated by a pedimented central bay and corner pavilions with pyramid roofs. The main rooms retain their Georgian decoration, with rich stucco ceilings. The council has struggled to acquire and reinstate the original St John pictures and furnishings, and even dares a plaster effigy of 'Hooter' St John at his desk in the library. A concession to showmanship is the numerous teddy bears strewn about the rooms for children to count.

The dining room is laid for dessert, with what remains of the St Johns' own tea and coffee service. The drawing room still has its 18th-century damask flock wallpaper, and the ceiling is a copy of Inigo Jones's ceiling from the Queen's House at Greenwich. An oddity is the state bedroom. This was previously the ballroom and part of its ceiling is delightfully Rococo. The picture frames, painted grey, are said to derive from the colour used by the St Johns when told they could not afford regilding.

The gem of the house is a 17th-century Huguenot painted window in the boudoir, made of quarries depicting rural and mythical scenes. Here too are pictures by an 18th-century Lady Diana Spencer, wife of the 2nd Viscount, whose speciality was cupids and the like. Her own portrait hangs here and she is strikingly similar to her relation.

Marlborough: Merchant's house

★★ Mid-17th-century town house with painted interiors

132 High Street, Marlborough; museum, open part year

In April 1653, a Marlborough tanner who had 'professed himself to be Christ' found his house consumed by fire. A strong wind carried the flames throughout the town, destroying 250 properties. In the recent Civil War, Marlborough had supported Cromwell, who duly organized a national collection to help in rebuilding. This took place swiftly. Within a year the diarist John Evelyn could declare the place 'now new built'.

There are few buildings intact from this period. One is the Merchant's House on the north side of the High Street. The building is timber-framed and tile-hung, with three bold gables surmounting its third storey. It was a branch of W. H. Smith until acquired in 1991 by the council and given to a trust. This is seeking to restore the interiors to their 1650s state, evidence for which miraculously remains in all eighteen rooms that will one day be on display.

The house belonged to a silk merchant, Thomas Bayly, and includes to its rear an extraordinary dining room. This was painted with vertical stripes to look like coloured silk wall-hangings, decoration which was admirably restored before English Heritage began meddling. The beefy, 17th-century staircase has carved balusters, matched by the same balusters painted on the walls. On the top flight are Italian cedar panels on built-in cupboards.

The first floor is one large panelled room with a bay window looking out over the market place. In its window pane is a stained-glass sundial, with a fly in its central panel, a play on the phrase, 'time flies'. The wide beamed floor is deliciously undulating, like the contours of a Wiltshire Down. The room cries out for furniture of the period.

The house is in severe danger of becoming a monument to conservationist pedantry. The trust battles against bureaucrats whose job seems to be to hinder not help those struggling to preserve old buildings. Original windows discovered in later walls cannot be restored and are absurdly represented by paint. The staircase murals have been restored only as fragments to give 'an impression' of the original and are so absurd as to be surreal. Some paintwork over fireplaces and round cornices has been reinstated, some has been 'conserved as found'. Grants are offered for education officers and project managers, not carpenters or painters. It is all mad.

This house, properly furnished and with its decoration reinstated, would be a superb example of a mid-17th century town house, to rank with the Red Lodge in Bristol or with Restoration House in Rochester (Kent). This will never happen while its custodians are crippled by red tape and London faddishness. Marlborough should revive the spirit of Cromwell.

Norrington manor

★★ A medieval hall house with 17th-century wing

Near Alvediston, 7 miles E of Shaftesbury; private house, open by appointment only

The old manor of Norrington lies secluded high on Cranborne Chase. It is invisible from a distance, nor can it see any other house. Here in deepest Wiltshire a medieval hall was built by the Gawen family in 1377, passing to the Wyndhams in 1658. A wing was added and the house bought by the Sykes family, its present owners, in 1952.

The first glimpse over the hill is a delight. Gothic windows mark the hall, with a medieval porch to the right and later wings projecting on both sides. The façade is pleasantly clothed in greenery. The porch contains a Gothic vault of tierceron ribs and a boss of a monster with its mouth open, a sophisticated carving.

The interior has been much altered. The screens passage has become an entrance hall and the hall a comfortable sitting room. Most interesting is the now derelict solar wing. This has been left agricultural, with an undercroft as richly vaulted as the porch. This could have been a chapel, storeroom or manorial treasury. There is a fragment of a Tudor stair tower outside. Above is the old parlour, with a large fireplace and windows, still displaying the dereliction that afflicted many English manors before 20th-century gentrification.

The other wing of the house, which would have contained the manorial offices, was rebuilt in the 17th century as the private house. The Sykes family, soldiers and farmers, take a lively interest in local history.

Above A deeply moulded arch frames the doorway to the 15th-century porch at Norrington. The porch leads to a small entrance hall then, on the left, to the medieval hall, one of only two parts of the Manor to survive from the 14th century.

Old Wardour castle

5 miles NE of Shaftesbury; English Heritage, open all year

Where would they be, these great fortified houses of England, had there been no Civil War? It led to the 'slighting' or destruction of hundreds of them. Yet without that war, some far worse cataclysm might have engulfed their custodians. France and Germany kept their châteaux and schlossen but later revolutions and wars left few in as good a state as those that survived in England.

Old Wardour is buried in the tumbling hills of Cranborne Chase. It looks across the valley to 18th-century New Wardour, now a monument to the stability that created the English Picturesque. The castle was built as a 'fortified residence' by Lord Lovel at the end of the 14th century, during the brief but dazzling reign of Richard II. At the time, courtiers' residences were harking back to a more chivalrous and romantic past.

The castle's plan was hexagonal, a shape derived from Burgundian castles of the Duc de Berry. It had a central Great Hall with symmetrical wings set at uniform angles, a form unusual in England at this early date. Overlooked by a hillside and composed entirely of vulnerable angles and walls, it was for show and not for war.

In 1547 the house was sold to a Cornish grandee, Sir Thomas Arundell, whose son Matthew reordered it, possibly with help from Robert Smythson, in the 1570s. Matthew enlarged the windows and inserted the larger chambers needed for Elizabethan entertainment.

The Arundells were Catholics and the house was besieged in the Civil War and bravely defended by Lady Blanche Arundell and her household, many of them women. Like Lady Bankes's defence of Corfe Castle (see page 26), such female heroism became the stuff of Royalist legend. One side of the castle collapsed through sapping during the siege.

The family moved to Breamore House (see page 76), not returning to a smaller house in the grounds until the 18th century. In 1769 the 8th Lord Arundell commissioned James Paine to build him a new house two miles away across a lake. The old castle formed the focal point in early landscaping by Capability Brown. The paying public were admitted as early as 1830. This view survives today. New Wardour is now a private residence, after half a century as Cranborne Chase, a girls' boarding school.

A surprising amount of the entrance front and outer walls of the castle survives. A corner turret, a fine Renaissance doorway and assorted fireplaces and tower rooms may all be admired. In the garden the 1773 Banqueting House is intact and used as a 'Victorian' tea-room. A grotto and fake stone circle complete the setting for what amounted to a true Georgian theme park.

Right At the heart of Old Wardour is an open courtyard, hexagonal in plan, as is the castle. At one side is the doorway to the main staircase, dignified by impressive Doric columns on either side and carved lions heads in the spandrels of the arch.

Philipps House

⭐ An austere example of Regency classicism

At Dinton, 8 miles W of Salisbury; National Trust, house open part year, park open all year

Philipps House does not get a good press. Its own National Trust guidebook uses such words as 'uninspired ... austere and unadorned', yet the drive across the estate is magnificent and the sight of the house in the distance is most picturesque. It was built in 1813 for the local squire, William Wyndham, by Sir Jeffry Wyatville. The house was sold to Bertram Philipps in 1917, from whom it passed to the Trust in 1943, becoming a YWCA hostel. The house is now privately tenanted, the main reception rooms being open to the public.

Philipps House is Wyatville at his most Soanian and severe. The exterior is a rectangular stone box, adorned with a simple Ionic portico. No vegetation is permitted to soften the exterior. Inside, the hall frieze offers a brief flourish of shells and cornucopia. Decorative exhaustion then sets in. The staircase hall demonstrates Wyatville's strongest suit, a flair for large spaces.

The whole house is arranged round this staircase. Its cold stone is almost surreal, with galleries hidden behind columned screens. The stair treads are thin and the space heated by vents from a basement furnace. This was so effective that a 19th-century Wyndham could write to her son that 'it is like living in the South of France and much more agreeable to me than a winter in Italy'.

Of the remaining rooms there is little to be said. The library has fine mahogany bookcases but little effort has been made by the National Trust or its tenants to bring things to life. Regency classicism is a style that requires opulence in its fittings.

SALISBURY
King's house

⭐ Medieval palace of the abbots of Sherborne

65 The Close, Salisbury; museum, open all year

The ghost of a grey lady is said to haunt the north staircase of the King's House. The same ghost should haunt a house in Des Moines, Iowa, home of the Weeks family, cosmeticians.

The Weekses visited the King's House in 1922 and so liked it that they decided to re-create it, to the inch, as their American home. They spent $1,500,000 stripping this and other Salisbury houses of panelling and antiques, which their owners were happy to sell. The Des Moines facsimile building is now a museum. So is the King's House. I imagine I would prefer Iowa's. What a poor comment this is on English civic pride.

This was one of the finest medieval palaces in The Close, belonging to the abbots of Sherborne. Their signature, Ham stone, can be seen on the façade. Seized by the Crown (hence the name) on the Dissolution, it was leased to secular tenants until 1851, when it became a training college for schoolmistresses.

This closed in 1978 and, like the nearby Wardrobe, use as a museum became the house's salvation. No attempt has been made to retain the different character of the rooms. To see any traces of the old house, one must peer behind display cases and boards.

Yet the house is still magnificent. The exterior is richly medieval. A porch with a fan vault is to the left of the two-gabled Great Hall. A large solar and parlour wing stands to the right. The chief surviving features date from the Jacobean period. There is an original staircase with, upstairs, geometrical ceiling plasterwork and a good frieze in the Abbot's Chamber. One of the motifs is a Red Indian chief beneath a pilgrim's scallop shell. I wonder how many Cree Indians made it to Santiago de Compostela.

The Close, Salisbury, runs around the edge of Cathedral Green. At one corner it skirts Choristers' Green (to the left, below), where Mompesson House claims a central position. Close by, at the corner of both greens, sits The Wardrobe. The King's House is further down the Close, opposite the cloisters. To the north, on the corner of St John Street, is Malmesbury House, obscured here by the Cathedral's towering spire.

SALISBURY

Malmesbury house

Below A view of Malmesbury House from the road. The sundial was added by James Harris III in 1749. The quotation is from *Hamlet*.

★ William-and-Mary mansion with Gothick interiors

15 The Close, Salisbury; private house, can be seen from road

SALISBURY

Malmesbury House is picture-book William-and-Mary. Hidden down an alley in the northeast corner of The Close, it was built by a member of the Harris family as an extension to a former canonry. In 1698 James Harris commissioned Wren's assistant, Alexander Fort, to extend the previous 17th-century building with a seven-bay façade overlooking a private garden. The exterior is an exquisite composition of silvery-white stone beneath a hat of jutting eaves and a single, assertive dormer. The effect is almost Chinese. Two stone pipers play on either side of the door.

Harris's son, also James, had a house in Twickenham near Horace Walpole's Strawberry Hill. Mesmerized by Walpole's stylistic eclecticism, Harris redecorated some of his interiors in the same Gothick style. The family later became Earls of Malmesbury and their Salisbury house languished, until bought in 1968 by a Conservative MP, the late John Cordle, who was the owner of the house on my visit.

The Georgian redecoration is immediately apparent in the spacious entrance hall, furnished with Napoleonic chairs upholstered with lions,

each with an individual expression. The walls are a soft Wedgwood blue with plasterwork rising up the spacious staircase, with shallow 'Queen Anne' treads. The dining room has a mildly Rococo ceiling on a terracotta background. It is hung with paintings of Cordle ancestors.

Upstairs, a bedroom is named after Charles II who stayed here when escaping the plague in 1665. He is said to have looked down on St John Street from the rear oriel window and been appalled at the poverty below. The admirable monarch called for his horse and rode through the town to boost morale. Over the fireplace is a rare Georgian display stand, decorative shelves designed to hold precious objects. Opposite is Handel's Room, used by the composer when performing in the former chapel next door. The ceiling contains the Harris family emblem of hedgehogs, a play on the French for hedgehog, *hérisson*, the nearest they could get to 'Harris and Son'.

The prize of Malmesbury House is the library, directly above the drawing room. This is one of the most delightful Gothick rooms I know. The plasterwork is like icing sugar, teased and moulded into ogees and crockets on every surface. The plaster is white, then gilded and set on pastel backgrounds. The ogee is repeated in arches, bookcases and the Rococo chimneypiece. The handling of the window alcove, with ribbed and crocketed vaulting, is supreme. The guide dates this work to 1740, but this is ten years before Walpole began Strawberry Hill. It must be later.

At the end of the lawn, next to a truly monumental hedge, is a pretty classical Orangery. In its pediment is said to be a secret chamber for hiding Royalists.

Mompesson house

★★ Elegant town house with Baroque-style frontispiece and Georgian interiors

Choristers' Green, The Close, Salisbury; National Trust, open part year

The smartest of the houses round The Close was built in 1701 for Charles Mompesson, lawyer and local MP. It was tenanted by the Townsend family until 1939 when the last representative, Barbara Townsend, died at the age of ninety-six. She was a celebrated figure in The Close, with her sketching equipment, large hats and gigantic shawls. The house served briefly as the residence of the bishop, but passed in 1952 to the National Trust. It is beautifully presented but lacks domesticity; it badly needs another Miss Townsend.

The façade to The Close is that of a handsome town mansion at the turn of the 18th century. Its designer may be the same as that of the exterior of Malmesbury House (see page 169), although here in more elegant, even ornamental, vein. Mompesson has a more Baroque frontispiece, with a broken pediment over the door and dentilated eaves. It now boasts a splendid magnolia.

The rooms are conventionally Georgian, dating from the 1740s. The entrance hall was described in 1913 as 'a great clutter of chairs, tables, coat stands, rugs and shawls, with pot plants massed in the corners ... the walls hung with pictures from cornice to dado'. This is sadly no more. A bold arch with floral spandrels gives onto the house's best feature, the staircase hall. The large stucco panels seem to demand large paintings. In the ceiling is a depiction of King Midas with ass's ears. The wide staircase has spiral balusters.

Of the downstairs rooms, the best is the drawing room, with an elaborate ceiling and overmantel. The dining room table is Hepplewhite, the china Sèvres, and the drinking glasses 18th-century. Upstairs is the elegant Green Room, hung with black-and-white portrait prints. Outside it is a display of Miss Townsend's watercolours.

Above left The main rooms at Mompesson were redecorated in grand style in the 1740s by Charles Longueville, brother-in-law of Charles Mompesson. It was Longueville who was responsible for the elaborate marble fireplace and overmantel in the drawing room.
Above Longueville also commissioned the ornate stucco decoration in the entrance hall and on the great archway that leads through to the staircase hall.

SALISBURY

The Wardrobe

⭐ A medieval mansion with fine Georgian Rococo decoration inside

58 The Close, Salisbury; museum, open part year

Too few of the houses round The Close are accessible to the public. What was the bishop's storehouse was disused on Pevsner's visit in 1975 and was then all but gutted for a regimental museum. Its modern display cases and institutional seats diminish its character as a historic building – though not totally.

The Wardrobe's façade is enticing. The central hall range, dating in part from 1254, was rebuilt in the 15th century. To this were added prominent gabled wings. A small entrance arcade leads into the ground floor, with a large Tudor window lighting the main room above. Much of this was altered in 1633 and then Victorianized.

The most diverting feature of the interior is a reordering that must have taken place in the mid-18th century, presumably to upgrade the building as a residence. Handsome fireplaces were inserted, for instance in the rear saloon. Unusual papier mâché Rococo decoration was applied to ceilings and walls. This is of a simple design, as if run up quickly by the plasterer's mate, but is rich and enjoyable, especially on the staircase. Behind the house is a peaceful garden (below) with a fine copper beech.

Stourhead

★ ★ ★ An English Palladian mansion set in magnificent landscaped grounds

At Stourton, 6 miles NE of Wincanton; National Trust, house open part year, gardens open all year

'The **garden** at Stourhead is a **masterpiece** of English landscape, **casual** yet **contrived**, **natural** yet **architectural**.'

Sir Henry Hoare, owner of Stourhead in the 1940s, had a difficult war. Finding his staff establishment depleted by conscription, he bombarded the War Office with letters. He demanded that the authorities at least supply him with the 'bare minimum' necessities of life – a cook, a butler, a maid and anyone 'properly qualified to polish silver vases with peacock feathers'. He was quite happy to accept evacuees provided they were qualified. Surely Whitehall should put its shoulder to the wheel? Did it not realize 'there is a war on'?

The house was built in 1720–24 for another Henry Hoare, a banker, at a time when English Baroque was giving way to English Palladian. The architect was Colen Campbell, doyen of the Palladians. Campbell had just designed Burlington House in London's Piccadilly and Wanstead in Essex for another banker, Richard Child. Hoare's son was 'Henry the Magnificent', banker to the Burlington set. He was a Medician figure, filling the house with works by Poussin, Mengs and Rysbrack. Extended by Colt Hoare in the 1790s, Stourhead was then mercifully left alone until transferred to the National Trust in 1946.

The house today looks warm and Italianate in a summer sun. Campbell's entrance portico (not built until 1838) is a serene essay in Palladian proportion. Steps lead up from each side, flanked by large eagles, the Hoare emblem, drinking from the stone basins. The façade would have the charm of Chiswick House, in west London, were it not flanked, and inevitably weakened, by wings erected at the end of the 18th century.

The interiors of the central block were lost in a fire in 1902 but were restored facsimile. They can seem cold and forbidding. Hoares still live on the estate and tenant part of the house, but the place

Above When Henry Hoare, 'the Magnificent', built Stourhead in the 1740s, his plans encompassed a sublime landscaped garden. Hoare was inspired by painted views of Italy and he wanted to create a series of eye-catching vistas throughout the garden. The River Stour was dammed to create the great lake, and the eye is drawn across the water to the Temple of Flora, the Palladian bridge and the old parish church of St Andrew.

badly needs a Marquess of Bath (see Longleat, page 154). The entrance hall is a handsome cube, reconstructed after the fire with broken pediments above the doorcases and fireplace. It is hung from floor to ceiling with Hoare portraits arranged, according to Colt Hoare in the early 19th century, to 'remind us of the genealogy of our families and recall to our minds the hospitality of its former inhabitants'. The finest work is an equestrian portrait of Henry the Magnificent, jointly by Michael Dahl and John Wootton.

The Regency library wing was designed by Colt Hoare himself and is one of the finest of its date (1792) in England. It has a dramatic barrel vault running the length of the room and is decorated with paintings of classical scenes. The bookcases are recessed into the olive green walls. The furniture includes a magnificent desk made, apparently on the spot, by the younger Thomas Chippendale, its pilasters portraying philosophers.

The Little Dining Room has a white Corinthian screen above red walls and carpet and is still used by the family. Behind the hall is the saloon. This was intended as a chapel but was soon pressed into service for 'county balls, theatricals, concerts and other entertainments ... essential to all country houses of consequence'. After the 1902 fire, it was refashioned as an Edwardian drawing room,

Above The Regency library, which mercifully escaped the 1902 fire at Stourhead, was built in 1792 by Messrs Moulton and Atkinson of Salisbury. The marble chimneypiece and early 18th-century plaster overmantel were brought from Wavendon, the Hoare family house in Buckinghamshire, and installed in their current position in 1913.

marked by heavy picture frames and ferns. When the National Trust restored it, the red wallpaper shocked the decorator, John Fowler, who told James Lees-Milne that it looked like a 'Bewlay-House pipe shop'. That, came the reply, was precisely the intention.

The Italian Room was once the state bedroom, the pretty Gothick bed alcove now filled with copies of Old Masters. The Cabinet and picture gallery are used to display the Hoares' principal pictures and furniture. The cabinet in the first room is an exquisite work of 17th-century Italian craftsmanship, covered in *pietra dura* and used to house precious gems and cameos. These rooms are hung with English landscapes and Old Masters, among them Poussin's *The Choice of Hercules*. Carlo Maratta's colloquy of *The Marchese Pallavicini and the Artist* embodies the Georgian ideal of the cultivated country gentleman.

The garden at Stourhead is a masterpiece of English landscape, casual yet contrived, natural yet architectural. In autumn, when the leaves are turning, the different shades of red and green round the serpentine lake are sublime. Henry Hoare began laying out the gardens with the help of Henry Flitcroft in the 1740s. He immediately opened it to the public and found it a sensational success, so much so that he had to build a hotel for visitors. A magazine declared, 'Prepare the mind for something grand and new/ For Paradise soon opens to the view!'

Swindon: Railway cottage

☆ Terraced cottage on a model estate of homes built for railway workers

Part of the STEAM Museum, Kemble Drive, Swindon; open for group tours by appointment only

Above Fortunate workers on the Great Western Railway ('God's Wonderful Railway', as it was also known) were housed in this model village. One cottage – next to the chapel on the far left of the picture – has been preserved. Below The parlour in the cottage looks much as it would have in GWR's Victorian heyday. The room would have been used only on special occasions.

When the great railway works at Swindon closed in the 1980s, it left the largest area of covered factory in Europe. The government duly demolished it, leaving some 'historic' walls as memorials. A railway museum now makes some effort to compensate, as does the walk through the old workers' tunnel to the model village. This remarkably intact estate was designed by Sir Matthew Digby Wyatt in the 1850s, for workers on the Great Western Railway, built by Brunel.

The village is a neighbourhood of pale stone cottages laid out on a grid, with school, chapel and institute. They still have the decorum of Georgian town planning. For train drivers and other skilled workers and supervisors, the cottages were substantial. They were handsome terraces, with small front gardens and rear access along alleys. One has been preserved in its original state, the others are occupied.

The cottage is extraordinarily evocative. The ground floor has parlour, dining room and kitchen, furnished with the usual Victorian household objects. The floors are covered in lino and rag rugs. The tables are littered with oil lamps, a Bible, Staffordshire pottery.

Westwood manor

★★★ Medieval manor house with Jacobean refurbishments

At Westwood, 5 miles SE of Bath; National Trust, open part year

Westwood is one of the manor houses that caught the eye of Edward Hudson of *Country Life* and his conservationists in the early years of the 20th century. Without their dedication, the West Country would be poorer by far. At the time, these houses may have seemed no different from thousands of run-down farms across England. Hudson made their renaissance a scholarly crusade.

Westwood belonged to a family of clothiers, the Hortons then Farewells, into the 18th century, when cloth gave way to agriculture as source of local wealth. The house became a farm. In 1911 it was acquired by a retired diplomat and Fellow of the Society of Antiquaries, Edgar Lister. He filled the house with panelling and internal porches, rescued from demolitions elsewhere. Tudor and Jacobean furniture came too and the floors were covered with oriental carpets. Lister left the house to the National Trust in 1956.

The house forms a picturesque group near Bradford-on-Avon, sandwiched between a medieval barn and a church. It is medieval in form, the exterior of stone and render, L-shaped with an original stair turret in the angle of the L. The old house had been comprehensively refurbished by

Above centre and right The King's Room was being used as a kitchen when Edgar Lister rescued Westwood in 1911 and began his sympathetic restoration. The plasterwork is original; it has been tentatively dated to just after the union of England and Scotland in 1603, from the roses and thistles in the overmantel decoration. Lister had the walls of the room lined with panelling taken from Keevil Manor, an Elizabethan house some 5 miles east of Westwood.

John Farewell at the start of the 17th century, and it is this period that dominates the interior. Farewell inserted a Great Parlour above the old hall.

A porch leads into the modest hall on the left, while on the right are two charming small rooms where once would have been kitchens. The name of the rear King's Room probably refers to its use for a manorial court. It has extensive Jacobean plasterwork on the ceiling and, round the fireplace, Red Indians, totem poles and a two-tailed mermaid, fashionable Jacobean emblems. In addition, Lister imported wall panelling painted with the kings and queens of England. The day-bed is covered in flame-stitch, executed by Lister himself, a skilled needleworker.

Lister was an enthusiast for early keyboard music and turned the Great Parlour into the present music room. Its coved plaster ceiling is covered in huge acanthus fronds. His furniture is dark and polished, its upholstery embroidered by himself. The west wing contains the old dining room and, upstairs, the Panelled Room and Oriel Room. These have been immaculately restored. Much of the panelling and the rare internal draught porches were acquired from a house in Bristol.

Wilton house

★★★★★ A Palladian palace with interiors by Inigo Jones and James Wyatt

At Wilton, 3 miles W of Salisbury; private house, open part year

Wilton is one of the great houses of England. The old nunnery was granted to a Welshman, William Herbert, by Henry VIII in 1544 on Herbert's marriage to Catherine Parr's sister. Herbert thus became, briefly, the King's brother-in-law. The house came with a huge estate of 46,000 acres and, eventually, the Earldom of Pembroke. Herberts were to be powers in the land and patrons of the arts. The 2nd Earl sponsored Shakespeare, while his wife, Mary Sidney, scholar and adored sister of the dazzling Sir Philip, was 'the greatest patroness of wit and learning of any lady in her time'. She was also an early breeder of horses. It was her second son, the 4th Earl, who employed

'... the Palladian bridge ... **presides quietly** over lake, house and grounds.'

John Webb in 1647 to implement plans for rebuilding the earlier house, first prepared by his mentor, Inigo Jones. The family founded the Wilton carpet factory, were prominent in the Burlington circle in the 18th century and supported Florence Nightingale in the 19th. The house has been well restored. Rooms have taped music, adding to their enjoyment; modern sculptures dot the gardens.

Visitors are greeted with a trumpet blast worthy of Blenheim. In 1801, James Wyatt moved Sir William Chambers's triumphal arch from a distant hill and placed it bang in front of the courtyard. It brings the house towards the town and gives the approach to Wilton a taste of imperial France. Despite that, the house exterior is unpompous. It is square built, like Lacock Abbey (see page 146) and Syon House, on the nunnery remains. The south front facing the lake is by Inigo Jones and his pupil John Webb in 1648. Each corner is crowned with a small gabled pavilion which seems not to know which way to face.

The character of much of Wilton's interior is due to James Wyatt. Entry to the house is into Wyatt's Gothic north front, presided over by a statue of Shakespeare copied from William Kent's in Westminster Abbey. Steps lead up to the cloisters, inserted by Wyatt in honour of Wilton's monastic

Left The 9th Earl of Pembroke (1692–1750) was a friend of the influential Palladian architects Lord Burlington and William Kent. In 1737 the Earl had the Palladian bridge built to create an architectural link between Wilton House and the wider landscaped grounds beyond. The River Nadder was widened above the bridge, then dammed to create a lake.

The paintings at Wilton are among the greatest treasures that the house has to offer. In the Corner Room is the *Interior of a Picture Gallery* (**above**), one of the first paintings to depict an art gallery, by the Flemish artist Frans Francken the Younger (1581–1642). In the Great Ante-Room hangs *Rembrandt's Mother* (**above right**), painted by the artist around 1629 and portraying her reading a large book. The same room also displays a Holbein portrait of Edward VI (**far right**); the 1st Earl of Pembroke was appointed one of the young King's guardians on the death of Edward's father, Henry VIII, in 1547. **Below right** The large group portrait of the 4th Earl and his family, painted c1635 by Anthony van Dyck, hangs on the west wall of Double Cube Room; the Earl commissioned both the room and the painting.

past. Courtyard windows flood its galleries with light. Wyatt thus offers a delicate Gothic hors d'oeuvre to the Italianate splendours ahead. Two smoking rooms survive from the earlier house, with simple classical fireplaces. The Large Smoking Room contains Chippendale's Violin Bookcase, so-called for the carved instruments above the central Rococo roundel, an exquisite work. The Little Ante-Room contains some of Wilton's finest small pictures, by Teniers, Poussin and van Goyen.

Wilton's tempo quickens with the six great state rooms of the Jones/Webb front. Here Jones sought his celebrated contrast: 'Outwardly every wise man carries a gravity, yet inwardly has his imagination set on fire and sometimes licentiously flies out.' Wilton is as good as his word. In these voluptuously decorated rooms, white plaster is encrusted with gold decoration. Bold red walls and pink carpets offer a backdrop to glorious paintings.

The Corner Room has Prince Rupert by Honthorst in pride of place over the mantelpiece, surrounded with works by Claude, Rubens, del Sarto and Hals. The Colonnade Room was converted for a visit of George III and has a phenomenal French Rococo ceiling of the 1730s by Andien de Clermont. Here hangs a serene Reynolds of Elizabeth Spencer. In the Great Ante-Room is a portrait

of Rembrandt's mother and a gentle depiction of the hapless Edward VI by Holbein.

Now comes the explosion. Jones's Double Cube Room is English architecture shaking off medieval inhibition and joining the European mainstream. The chamber is 60ft by 30ft. The overmantel is flanked by garlanded pendants, as are the great doors. The coving, painted in the 1650s by Edward Pierce, depicts urns, fruit and cherubs. In the ceiling are set three Baroque paintings. The fastidious Sacheverell Sitwell found not all about this room to his taste. 'The carving heavy and not equal to the best Italian work,' he said, but accepted that this may be inevitable in a room of this grandeur.

The room was designed by Jones to take the van Dyck paintings that fill the wall panels. The largest is a stunning work of the 4th Earl and his family, arrayed in a variety of flamboyant poses like models on a catwalk. They seem about to step out of the frame and parade across the carpet below. The room is furnished mostly by Kent and Chippendale.

It is regrettable that, on the tour, the visitor reaches the Single Cube Room after the Double, the opposite being Jones's intention. The result is slight anticlimax. The decorative scheme is the same, with white painted panelling enriched with gold leaf. The coving is less aggressively decorated, more classical and harmonious.

The Upper Cloisters offer yet more of Wilton's art collection, including two Brueghels and Samuel Scott's views of London, including of Jones's first Covent Garden development. The windows look down on a new knot garden. In the grounds, the Palladian bridge by Roger Morris has been restored and continues to preside quietly over lake, house and grounds alike.